MY WORLD
ATLAS

Discovery**KIDS**.com

This edition published by Parragon Books Ltd in 2015 and distributed by Parragon Inc.
440 Park Avenue South, 13th Floor
New York, NY 10016
www.parragon.com

Please retain this information for future reference.

ISBN 978-1-4723-9841-3

Printed in Malaysia

MY WORLD
ATLAS

PaRRagon

Bath • New York • Cologne • Melbourne • Delhi
Hong Kong • Shenzhen • Singapore • Amsterdam

CONTENTS

CENTRAL AMERICA AND THE CARIBBEAN

SOUTH AMERICA

THE AMERICAS

ASIA

OCEANIA

AFRICA

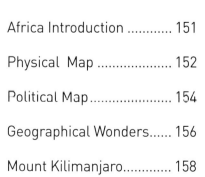

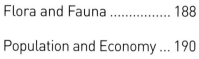

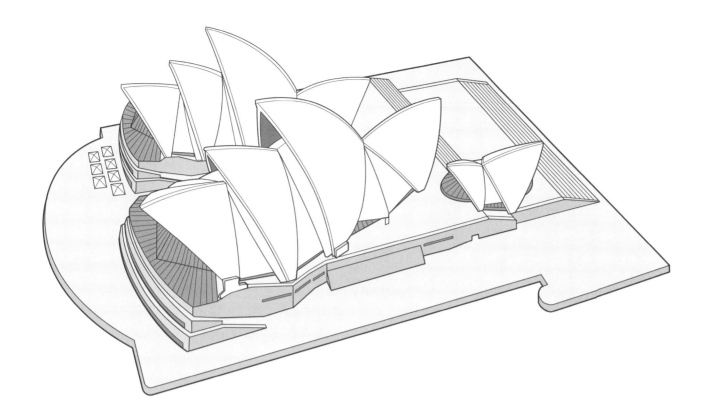

THE WORLD IN FIGURES

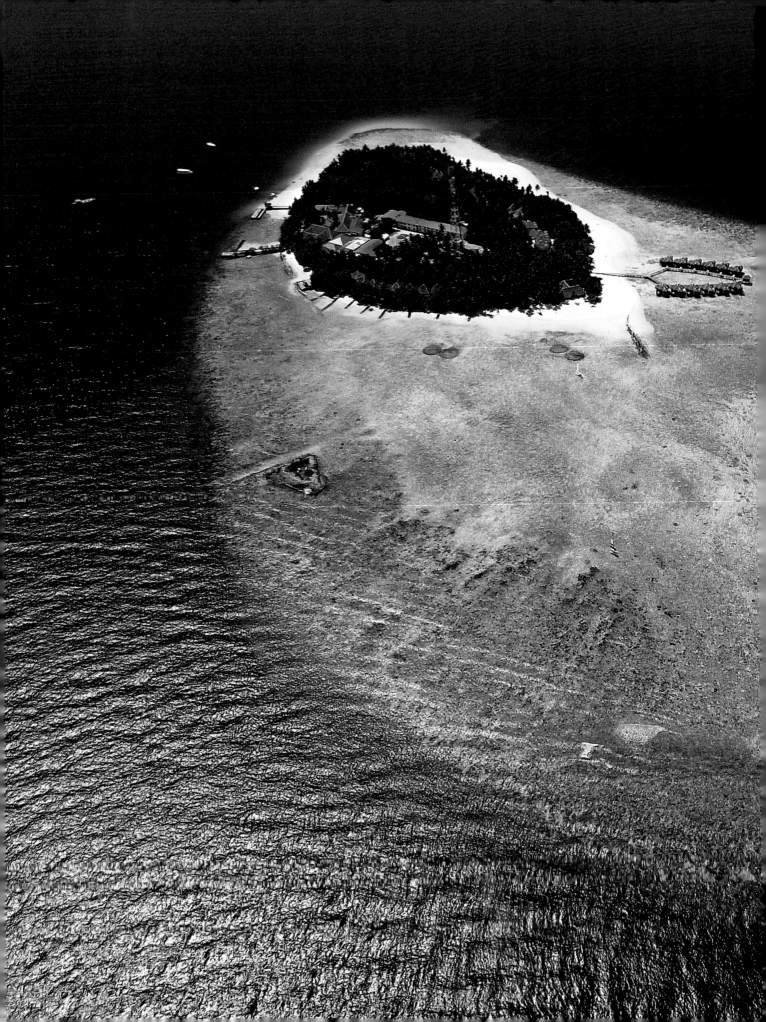

INTRODUCTION

Our planet is an amazing place!

Its seas and oceans are full of incredible plants and animals, from tiny coral to enormous whales.

On land, the scenery ranges from scorching deserts and fertile plains to soaring mountains. These fantastic features have been formed over millions of years by the powerful forces of plate tectonics and the continual action of wind, rain, ice, snow, and heat.

This book will take you on an amazing journey through the continents, showing the natural features found in each of them. It will also reveal who lives there and some of the wonderful sites created by humankind.

There is a helpful glossary on pages 218–219 and you will find these words in bold in the main text.

TROPICAL PARADISE
THIS CORAL ATOLL, SURROUNDED BY A SHALLOW LAGOON, SHOWS ONE
OF THE CHAIN OF 1300 SMALL ISLANDS THAT MAKE UP THE MALDIVES.

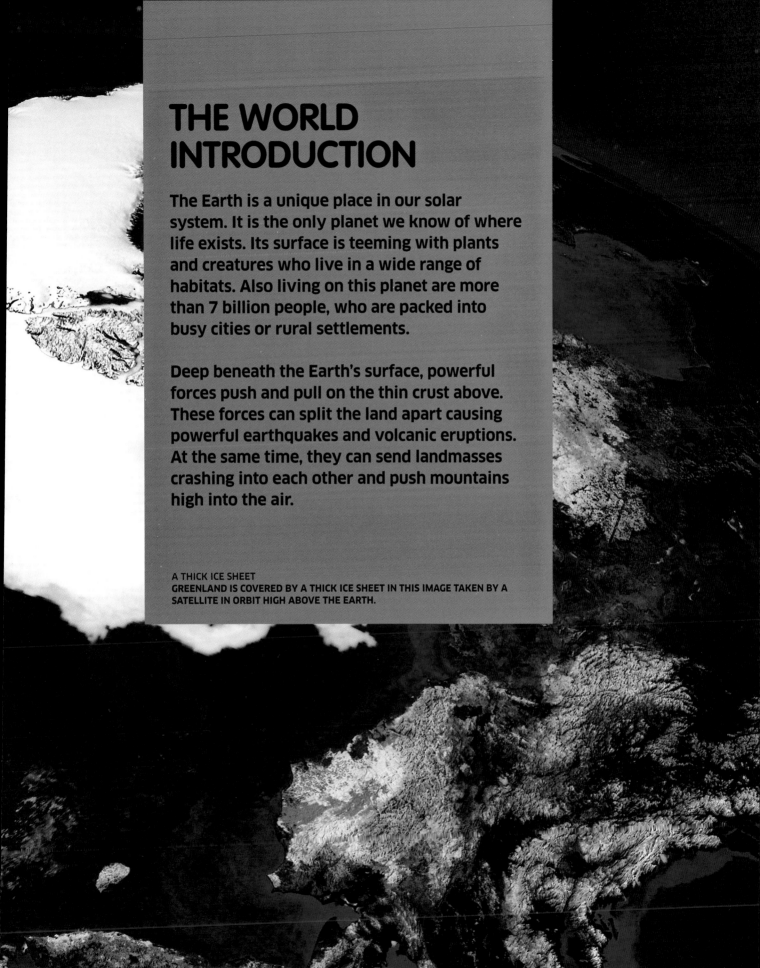

THE WORLD
INTRODUCTION

The Earth is a unique place in our solar system. It is the only planet we know of where life exists. Its surface is teeming with plants and creatures who live in a wide range of habitats. Also living on this planet are more than 7 billion people, who are packed into busy cities or rural settlements.

Deep beneath the Earth's surface, powerful forces push and pull on the thin crust above. These forces can split the land apart causing powerful earthquakes and volcanic eruptions. At the same time, they can send landmasses crashing into each other and push mountains high into the air.

A THICK ICE SHEET
GREENLAND IS COVERED BY A THICK ICE SHEET IN THIS IMAGE TAKEN BY A SATELLITE IN ORBIT HIGH ABOVE THE EARTH.

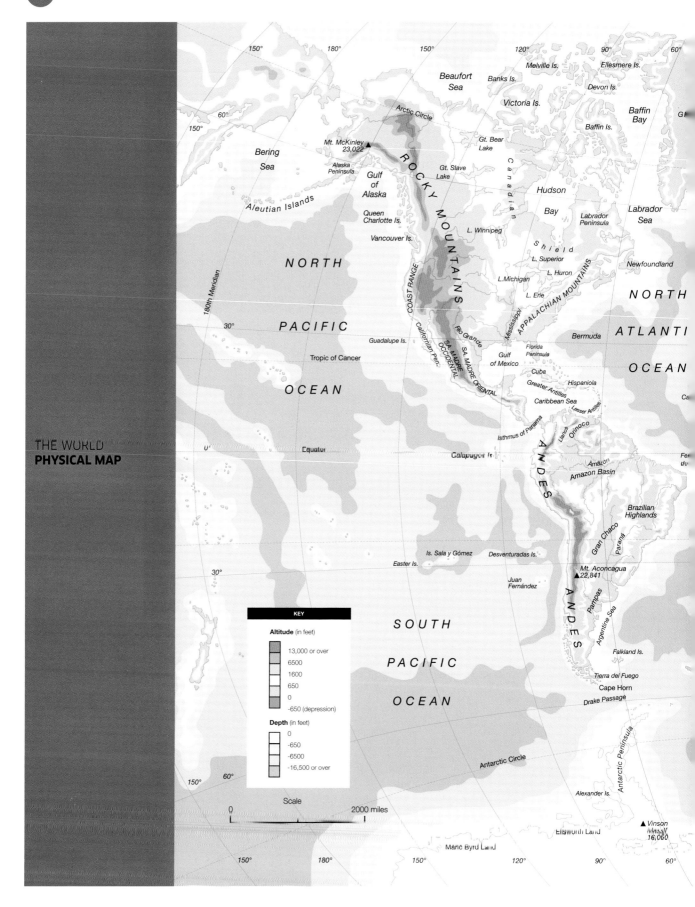

THE WORLD
PHYSICAL MAP

150° 180° 150° 120° 90° 60°

Melville Is.
Ellesmere Is.

Beaufort
Sea
Banks Is.
Devon Is.

Victoria Is.
Baffin
Bay

60°
Arctic Circle
Gt. Bear
Lake
Baffin Is.

150°
Mt. McKinley
23,022
R O C K Y   M O U N T A I N S

Bering
Sea
Alaska
Peninsula
Gulf
of
Alaska
Gt. Slave
Lake
Hudson
Labrador
Peninsula
Labrador
Sea

Aleutian Islands
Queen
Charlotte Is.
L. Winnipeg
Bay
C a n a d i a n
S h i e l d
Newfoundland

Vancouver Is.
L. Superior

N O R T H
COAST RANGE
L.Michigan
L. Huron
A P P A L A C H I A N   M O U N T A I N S
N O R T H

180th Meridian
L. Erie

30°
P A C I F I C
Rio Grande
Mississippi
Bermuda
A T L A N T I

Guadalupe Is.
Californian Pen.
SA. MADRE
OCCIDENTAL
SA. MADRE ORIENTAL
Gulf
of Mexico
Florida
Peninsula
O C E A N

Tropic of Cancer
Cuba
Greater Antilles
Hispaniola
Ca

O C E A N
Caribbean Sea
Lesser Antilles

Isthmus of Panama
Llanos
Orinoco
A N D E S

0°
Equator
Galapagos Is.
Amazon
Fer
d

Amazon Basin

Brazilian
Highlands

Gran Chaco
Paraná

Is. Sala y Gómez
Desventuradas Is.

30°
Easter Is.
Mt. Aconcagua
22,841

Juan
Fernández
A N D E S
Pampas
Argentine Sea

KEY

Altitude (in feet)
S O U T H
Falkland Is.

13,000 or over
Tierra del Fuego

6500
P A C I F I C
Cape Horn

1600
Drake Passage

650
O C E A N

0

-650 (depression)
Antarctic Peninsula

Depth (in feet)
Antarctic Circle

0
Alexander Is.

-650

-6500

-16,500 or over

150°
60°

Scale

0
2000 miles
Ellsworth Land
Vinson
Massif
16,060

Marie Byrd Land

150° 180° 150° 120° 90° 60°

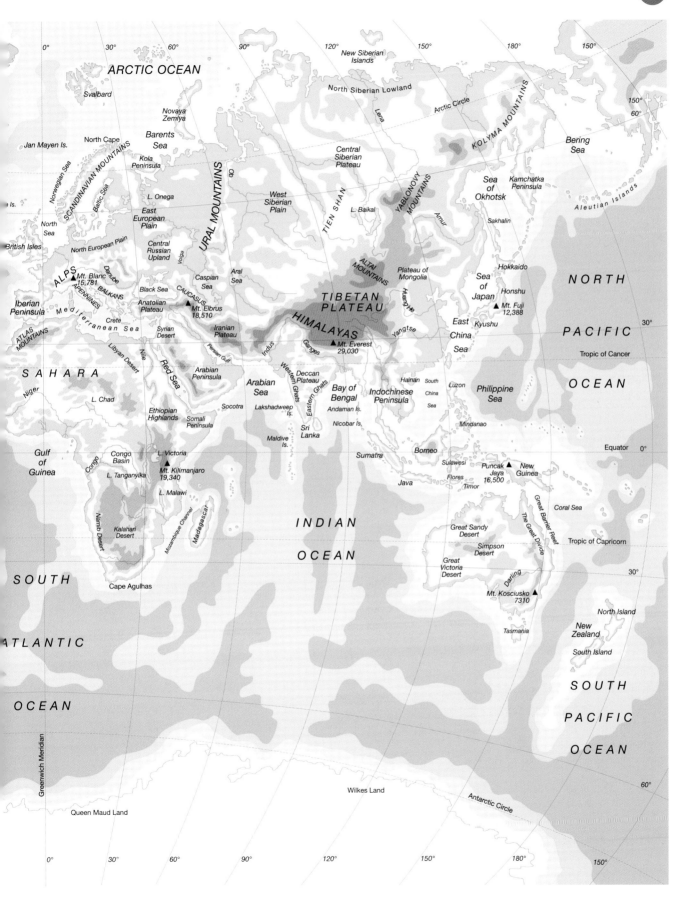

ARCTIC OCEAN

Svalbard

Jan Mayen Is.

North Cape

Novaya Zemlya

New Siberian Islands

North Siberian Lowland

Arctic Circle

KOLYMA MOUNTAINS

Bering Sea

Barents Sea

Kola Peninsula

Central Siberian Plateau

Sea of Okhotsk

Kamchatka Peninsula

Aleutian Islands

Norwegian Sea

SCANDINAVIAN MOUNTAINS

Baltic Sea

L. Onega

West Siberian Plain

TIEN SHAN

L. Baikal

YABLONOVY MOUNTAINS

Amur

Sakhalin

East European Plain

URAL MOUNTAINS

Ob

North Sea

North European Plain

Central Russian Upland

Volga

Caspian Sea

Aral Sea

ALTAI MOUNTAINS

Plateau of Mongolia

Huang He

Hokkaido

Sea of Japan

Honshu

NORTH

British Isles

ALPS
Mt. Blanc
15,781

APENNINES

BALKANS

Danube

Black Sea

CAUCASUS

Mt. Elbrus
18,510

TIBETAN PLATEAU

HIMALAYAS

Yangtse

Mt. Fuji
12,388

Kyushu

PACIFIC

Iberian Peninsula

Mediterranean Sea

Crete

Anatolian Plateau

Syrian Desert

Iranian Plateau

Indus

Ganges

Mt. Everest
29,030

East China Sea

30°

ATLAS MOUNTAINS

Libyan Desert

Red Sea

Persian Gulf

Western Ghats

Deccan Plateau

Eastern Ghats

Hainan

South China Sea

Luzon

Philippine Sea

OCEAN

Tropic of Cancer

SAHARA

Nile

Arabian Peninsula

Arabian Sea

Bay of Bengal

Indochinese Peninsula

Niger

L. Chad

Socotra

Lakshadweep Is.

Andaman Is.

Mindanao

Ethiopian Highlands

Somali Peninsula

Nicobar Is.

Sri Lanka

Maldive Is.

Sumatra

Borneo

Equator

0°

Gulf of Guinea

Congo

Congo Basin

L. Victoria

Mt. Kilimanjaro
19,340

Sulawesi

Puncak Jaya
16,500

New Guinea

L. Tanganyika

Flores

Timor

L. Malawi

Java

Great Barrier Reef

Coral Sea

INDIAN

Namib Desert

Mozambique Channel

Madagascar

Great Sandy Desert

The Great Divide

Kalahari Desert

Simpson Desert

Tropic of Capricorn

OCEAN

Great Victoria Desert

SOUTH

Cape Agulhas

30°

Darling

Mt. Kosciusko
7310

North Island

ATLANTIC

New Zealand

Tasmania

South Island

OCEAN

SOUTH

PACIFIC

OCEAN

60°

Greenwich Meridian

Wilkes Land

Antarctic Circle

Queen Maud Land

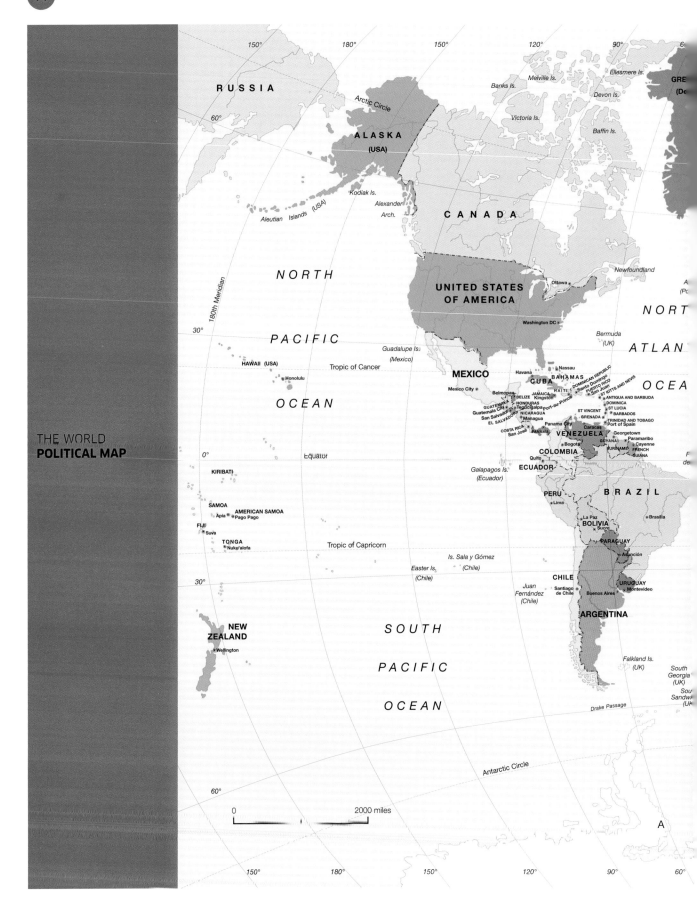

RUSSIA

Arctic Circle

60°

ALASKA
(USA)

Kodiak Is.

Aleutian Islands (USA)

Alexander Arch.

Melville Is.

Banks Is.

Victoria Is.

Devon Is.

Ellesmere Is.

Baffin Is.

GRE
(De

CANADA

NORTH

180th Meridian

30°

PACIFIC

OCEAN

HAWAII (USA)

Honolulu

Guadalupe Is.
(Mexico)

Tropic of Cancer

UNITED STATES
OF AMERICA

Washington DC

Ottawa

Newfoundland

A
(Po

NORT

ATLAN

Bermuda
(UK)

MEXICO

Mexico City

Havana

Nassau

CUBA

BAHAMAS

DOMINICAN REPUBLIC

Santo Domingo

OCEA

Belmopan
BELIZE

JAMAICA
Kingston

PUERTO RICO
San Juan

ST KITTS AND NEVIS

THE WORLD
POLITICAL MAP

0°

Equator

KIRIBATI

SAMOA

Apia
Pago Pago

AMERICAN SAMOA

FIJI
Suva

TONGA
Nuku'alofa

Tropic of Capricorn

GUATEMALA
Guatemala City
San Salvador
EL SALVADOR
COSTA RICA
San José

HAITI
port-au-Prince

HONDURAS
Tegucigalpa
NICARAGUA
Managua
PANAMA
Panama City

ANTIGUA AND BARBUDA
DOMINICA
ST LUCIA
BARBADOS
GRENADA
TRINIDAD AND TOBAGO
Port of Spain

ST VINCENT

Caracas
VENEZUELA

Georgetown
GUYANA
SURINAME

Paramaribo
Cayenne
FRENCH
GUIANA

Bogotá
COLOMBIA

Quito
ECUADOR

F
de

Galapagos Is.
(Ecuador)

PERU
Lima

BRAZIL

La Paz
BOLIVIA
Sucre

Brasília

Is. Sala y Gómez

Easter Is.
(Chile)

(Chile)

PARAGUAY
Asunción

CHILE

Santiago
de Chile

URUGUAY
Montevideo

Buenos Aires

Juan
Fernández
(Chile)

NEW
ZEALAND

Wellington

SOUTH

PACIFIC

OCEAN

30°

ARGENTINA

Falkland Is.
(UK)

South
Georgia
(UK)

Sou
Sandw
(UK

Drake Passage

60°

Antarctic Circle

0   2000 miles

A

150°   180°   150°   120°   90°   60°

ARCTIC OCEAN

Svalbard
(Norway)

ALASKA
(USA)

New Siberian Is.

Arctic Circle

Novaya
Zemlya

Jan Mayen Is.
(Norway)

Aleutian Islands (USA)

180th Meridian

NORTH

RUSSIA

Sakhalin

NORWAY
SWEDEN
FINLAND

Oslo
Stockholm
Helsinki
Tallinn
ESTONIA
Riga
LATVIA
LITHUANIA
RUSSIA
Vilnius

Moscow

PACIFIC

Hokkaido

DENMARK
Copenhagen
Minsk
Warsaw
BELARUS

UNITED
KINGDOM
Dublin
London
Amsterdam
Brussels
NETHERLANDS
Berlin
GERMANY
CZECH REP.
Bratislava
Vienna
POLAND
Kiev
UKRAINE

KAZAKHSTAN

Astana

Ulan Bator
MONGOLIA

Honshu

NORTH
KOREA
Pyongyang
Seoul
SOUTH
KOREA
JAPAN
Tokyo

IRELAND

FRANCE
Paris
SWITZERLAND
AUSTRIA
HUNGARY
Budapest
ROMANIA
MOLDOVA
Chisinau
Bucharest

Bishkek
KYRGYZSTAN
Tashkent
UZBEKISTAN
TAJIKISTAN

Beijing
CHINA

MONACO
ITALY
Corsica
(France)
Rome
Sardinia
(Italy)

Belgrade
Sofia
BULGARIA
GEORGIA
Tbilisi
ARMENIA
AZERBAIJAN
Yerevan
Baku

TURKMENISTAN
Ashgabat

Dushanbe

PORTUGAL
SPAIN
Lisbon
Madrid
Balearic Is.
(Spain)

GREECE
Athens
TURKEY
Ankara

Tehran

Islamabad

Taipei
TAIWAN

Tropic of Cancer

Rabat
MOROCCO

Algiers
Tunis
TUNISIA
Tripoli
Valletta
MALTA
Sicily
Crete
CYPRUS
Nicosia
Beirut
LEBANON
SYRIA
Damascus
ISRAEL
Jerusalem
Amman
JORDAN
Baghdad
IRAQ
IRAN

Kabul
AFGHANISTAN

New Delhi

Kathmandu
NEPAL
BHUTAN
Thimphu

OCEAN

30°

Ryukyu Is.

MAURITANIA
Nouakchott

ALGERIA
LIBYA
EGYPT
Cairo

Riyadh
Doha
QATAR
Abu Dhabi
UNITED
ARAB
EMIRATES
Muscat
KUWAIT
Kuwait City
PAKISTAN

INDIA

BANGLADESH
Dhaka
MYANMAR
(BURMA)
Hanoi

Luzon
Manila

PACIFIC

MALI
NIGER
CHAD
SUDAN
Khartoum
N'Djamena
ERITREA
Asmara
YEMEN
Sana
OMAN

SAUDI
ARABIA

Socotra
(Yemen)

Lakshadweep Is.
(India)

Andaman
Is.
(India)

Yangon
Vientiane
LAOS
THAILAND
Bangkok
VIETNAM
CAMBODIA
Phnom Penh

PHILIPPINES

Mindanao

PALAU
Koror

SENEGAL
Bamako
BURKINA
FASO
Niamey
Ouagadougou
NIGERIA
Abuja

GUINEA
SIERRA
LEONE
CÔTE
D'IVOIRE
Accra
Porto-Novo
Lagos

CENTRAL
AFRICAN REP.
Bangui
SOUTH
SUDAN
Juba
Addis Ababa
ETHIOPIA

SRI LANKA
Kotte

Nicobar
Is.
(India)

BRUNEI
Bandar Seri Begawan

CAMEROON
Yaoundé
Malabo
EQUATORIAL GUINEA
SÃO TOMÉ
& PRÍNCIPE
GABON
Libreville
DEMOCRATIC
REPUBLIC
OF THE
CONGO
Kinshasa
Brazzaville
CONGO

UGANDA
Kampala
KENYA
Nairobi
RWANDA
Kigali
BURUNDI
Bujumbura
TANZANIA
Dodoma

MALDIVES
Malé

SOMALIA
Mogadishu

MALAYSIA
KUALA LUMPUR
SINGAPORE
Borneo

Equator

Sulawesi

NAURU

0°

SEYCHELLES
Victoria

Jakarta
INDONESIA

PAPUA
NEW GUINEA
Port Moresby

SOLOMON
ISLANDS
Honiara

TUVALU

ANGOLA
Luanda
ZAMBIA
Lusaka
Lilongwe

COMOROS
Moroni

VANUATU
Port Vila
FIJI
Suva

NAMIBIA
Windhoek
BOTSWANA
Gaborone
ZIMBABWE
Harare
Pretoria
MOZAMBIQUE
MADAGASCAR
Antananarivo

Port Louis
MAURITIUS
Réunion
(France)

INDIAN

NEW
CALEDONIA
Nouméa

SOUTH
AFRICA
Cape Town
Maputo
SWAZILAND
Mbabane
LESOTHO
Maseru

OCEAN

Tropic of Capricorn

AUSTRALIA

30°

SOUTH

ATLANTIC

OCEAN

Canberra

NEW
ZEALAND

Wellington

SOUTH

PACIFIC

OCEAN

	COUNTRY	CAPITAL
1	MACEDONIA	Skopje
2	MONTENEGRO	Podgorica
3	BOSNIA HERZEGOVINA	Sarajevo
4	CROATIA	Zagreb
5	SLOVENIA	Ljubljana
6	SAN MARINO	San Marino
7	LIECHTENSTEIN	Vaduz
8	LUXEMBOURG	Luxembourg
9	ANDORRA	Andorra la Vella
10	KOSOVO	Pristina
11	BAHRAIN	Manama

ANTARCTICA

Antarctic Circle

Greenwich Meridian

THE EARTH'S MOVEMENTS

Like all the planets in the solar system, the Earth spins on its own axis and it also orbits the Sun. These two movements cause the difference between day and night and the changing of the seasons.

23.5°
The angle at which the Earth is tilted.

20/21 JUNE
The longest day in the northern hemisphere happens on the summer solstice.

Yearly Orbit

The Earth takes 365 days, 5 hours, and 48 minutes to orbit the Sun. As the Earth changes position, the seasons and the length of the day and night change, too. The winter solstice is the shortest day of the year, while the summer solstice is the longest day. At the equinoxes, day and night are of equal length all over the planet.

(NOT TO SCALE)

SUN

22/23 SEPTEMBER
This is the autumn equinox in the northern hemisphere. Day and night are both 12 hours long.

91.7 MILLION MILES

Axis of rotation

21/22 DECEMBER
This is the winter solstice in the northern hemisphere. It is the shortest day of the year.

Daily Rotation

The Earth turns around its own axis each day. This movement causes day and night. It also makes the planet slightly flattened at the poles and causes ocean currents.

94.8 MILLION MILES

20/21 MARCH
This is the spring equinox in the northern hemisphere. Day and night are the same length.

Hemispheres
The Earth is divided into two halves, or hemispheres: the northern hemisphere and the southern hemisphere. The equator is the imaginary line that separates them. When it is summer in the north, it is winter in the south.

Northern Hemisphere

Equator

Southern Hemisphere

LEAP YEAR
Every fourth year, the month of February has 29 days instead of 28. This is called a leap year.

Jet lag
Long-distance flights can cause jet lag. This is because a change in time zones can upset our body's natural rhythm.

Time Zones
The Earth is divided into 24 different time zones by imaginary lines that go from pole to pole. Each zone's time is one hour different from its neighbors, with the Greenwich Meridian at the center.

GREENWICH MERIDIAN

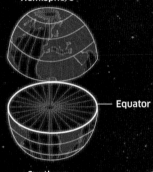

24:00 HOURS
West
East
3:00
21:00
6:00
18:00
N
9:00
15:00
12:00 HOURS

STRUCTURE OF THE EARTH

The Earth is very different under its surface. The rocky ground on which we live is only a thin crust. Underneath the crust is the mantle, made of solid and liquid rock, and in the center is a hot metal core. The whole planet is surrounded by a layer of gases that form the atmosphere.

Outer mantle
The movement of the outer mantle causes earthquakes and volcanoes.

385 MI

How Far Have We Explored?

It is more than 3958 miles from the surface to the center of the Earth. So far, we have managed to explore 7.5 miles down.

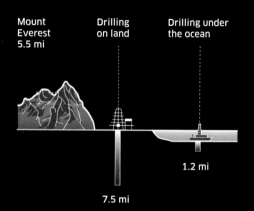

Mount Everest 5.5 mi

Drilling on land

Drilling under the ocean

1.2 mi

7.5 mi

1358 MI

1392 MI

Inner core
The inner core is made of solid iron and **nickel**.

(NOT TO SCALE)

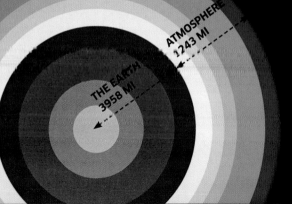

ATMOSPHERE 1243 MI

THE EARTH 3958 MI

Outer core
The outer core is made of molten iron and nickel.

Inner mantle
Heavy rocks make up the mantle. They have a temperature of more than 1832 °F.

EXOSPHERE

THERMOSPHERE

MESOSPHERE

STRATOSPHERE

TROPOSPHERE

HOT PLANET
The temperature
of the Earth rises
the closer you get
to the center.

The Atmosphere

**The atmosphere is made
up of a mixture of gases,
mainly nitrogen and
oxygen. It is divided
into different layers
depending on the amount
of gases at each height.
The atmosphere gives us
the air we breathe, and
it protects us from the
Sun's harmful rays.**

Crust
This outer
layer of rock is
4–43 miles thick.

Solar
radiation

Solar
radiation

No atmosphere
Without an
atmosphere, life would
be wiped out by the
radiation and heat.

Atmosphere
Filters the Sun's
rays and distributes
its heat.

The Hydrosphere

**The hydrosphere is the name for the
liquid part of the Earth, including the
oceans, lakes, rivers, groundwater,**
**and water in the atmosphere. Water
covers more than two-thirds of the
Earth's surface.**

LAND OR OCEAN?

TOTAL VOLUME OF WATER

FRESH WATER

29.2%
land

70.8%
water

97%
salt

3%
fresh

2.15%
groundwater

0.85% ice

0.01%
surface and
atmosphere

THE EARTH'S CRUST

The continents and oceans are found on the Earth's crust. This crust is made up of huge pieces that fit together like a jigsaw puzzle. They are called tectonic plates. These plates float on molten rock, or magma.

NEW ROCKS
When magma from a volcano cools, it forms new rocks in the Earth's crust.

Shaping the Earth's Crust

1 Folds
When two plates push together, they form folds. These folds are seen on the surface of the crust as mountains. The Alps, Andes, and Rockies are examples of **fold mountains**.

Continental drift
The tectonic plates are continually moving and can move as much as 4 inches each year. This movement is called **continental drift**.

2 Ridges
When two tectonic plates move apart, they leave a gap. This gap is filled with magma from inside the Earth. The magma hardens to form a ridge.

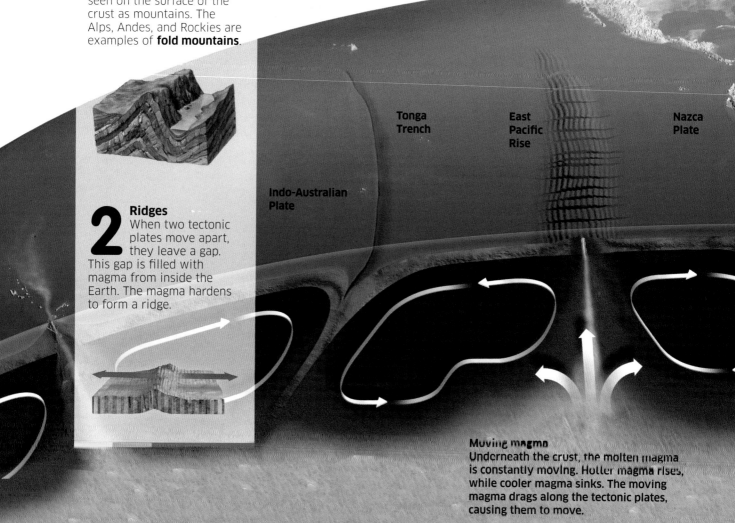

Tonga Trench

East Pacific Rise

Nazca Plate

Indo-Australian Plate

Moving magma
Underneath the crust, the molten magma is constantly moving. Hotter magma rises, while cooler magma sinks. The moving magma drags along the tectonic plates, causing them to move.

43 miles
The maximum thickness of the Earth's crust.

Fault Lines
The plates in the Earth's crust are separated along cracks called fault lines. The rock along a fault can move suddenly. When this happens, we feel the movement as an earthquake.

Tectonic Plates
The Earth's crust is made up of seven major tectonic plates plus several smaller ones.

The tectonic plates around North America

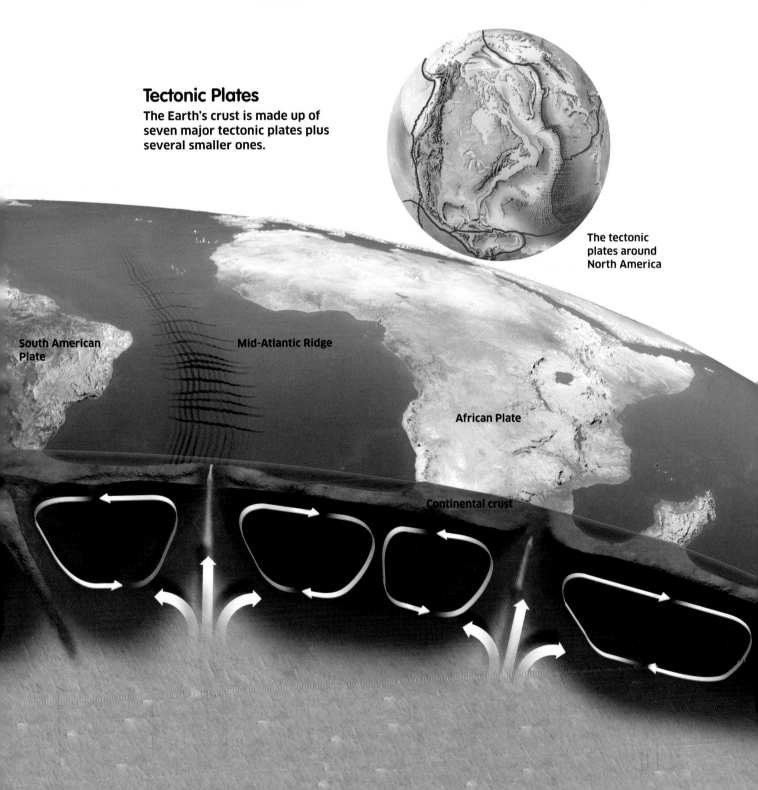

South American Plate

Mid-Atlantic Ridge

African Plate

Continental crust

THE OCEANS AND SEAS

Much of the Earth is covered by a large body of salt water, which surrounds the continents. The water forms large, deep oceans and smaller, shallow seas. Underneath the waves, there are huge underwater mountain ranges called ridges and deep valleys called trenches.

Trenches

The long, steep-sided valleys on the ocean floor are called trenches.

Arctic
Atlantic
Pacific
Indian
Southern

Five Oceans

Geographers divide the planet's water into five oceans: Pacific, Atlantic, Indian, Arctic, and Southern.

Aleutian Trench

About 2050 miles long and more than 24,934 feet deep, the Aleutian Trench is the world's largest.

Liquid Planet

Nearly 71 percent of the planet's surface is covered with water.

Pacific Ocean
Area: 63.8 million sq mi
Average depth: 14,000 ft

Atlanic Ocean
Area: 41 million sq mi
Average depth: 12,880 ft

Indian Ocean
Area: 29 million sq mi
Average depth: 12,760 ft

Arctic Ocean
Area: 5.42 million sq mi
Average depth: 3240 ft

Southern Ocean
Area: 7.85 million sq mi
Average depth: 3953 ft

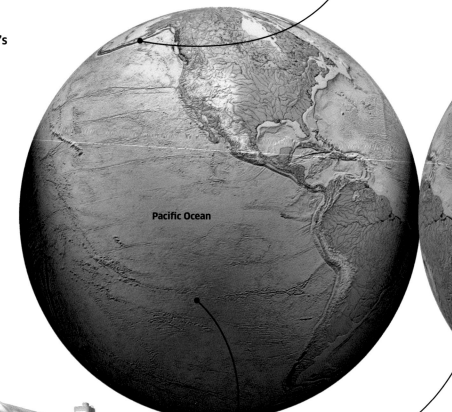

Pacific Ocean

The Deepest Descent

The Bathyscaphe Trieste holds the record for the deepest descent. In 1960, it went down to the Mariana Trench, 35,797 feet below sea level.

East Pacific Rise
The Galapagos Islands and Easter Island lie along this long ocean ridge.

Mid-Atlantic Ridge
This ridge crosses the Atlantic Ocean from north to south. Some of its mountains have emerged as volcanic islands, including the Azores and Ireland.

Ocean Life

Most of the planet's life is found in the oceans
and seas. The waters are home to life forms
ranging from the microscopic plankton to the
largest animals of all, whales.

CURRENTS
The ocean currents
are large masses of
cold or hot water
moving through
the oceans.

Blue whale
The largest animal on the
planet, the blue whale
(above), weighs between
100 and 120 tons.

Mariana Trench
Located in the Western Pacific,
the Mariana Trench reaches
36,201 feet in depth. It is the deepest
trench in the world.

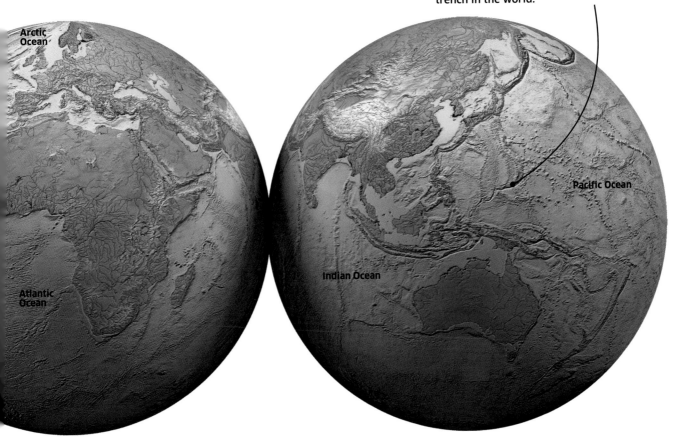

Arctic
Ocean

Atlantic
Ocean

Indian Ocean

Pacific Ocean

Types of Seas

Inland
These seas are
surrounded by
land, such as the
Caspian Sea.

Coastal
Coastal seas are
found in shallow
areas along
continents' coasts.

Continental
These seas are
between land
but have a channel
to the ocean.

THE ARCTIC

The Arctic is the region north of the Arctic Circle. This region includes the northern parts of Asia, North America, and Europe, together with most of the world's largest island, Greenland. These land areas enclose the world's smallest ocean, the Arctic Ocean. Near its ice-covered center is the North Pole.

Icebergs Icebergs break away from valley glaciers and from Greenland's huge ice sheet. Some drift south into the Atlantic Ocean.

The Inuit

The Inuit live in the Arctic region of North America. In 1999, a new Canadian province named Nunavut was established for them.

A Permanently Cold Region

The Arctic is a bitterly cold region and the Arctic Ocean is largely covered with thick ice throughout the year. Temperatures on the central **ice cap** can drop below -85 °F, but ocean currents keep the southwestern coast relatively mild.

Greenland

With the exception of Antarctica, Greenland is the world's least-populated land. As well as the Inuit of Greenland and northern Canada, other Arctic peoples are the Sami found in northern Scandinavia, and the Samoyeds, Tungus, and Yakuts of northern Asia.

18,176 ft
The depth of the Arctic Ocean at its deepest.

EXPEDITION
The first expedition to claim to have reached the North Pole was led by Commander Robert Peary in 1909, but many experts now doubt that he actually got there.

ALASKA (USA)
Yukon
Bering Strait
CHURCHI SEA
Ambarchik
Kolyma
Barrow • Pt. Barrow
Mackenzie
EAST SIBERIAN SEA
Indigirka
BEAUFORT SEA
C.BATHURST
New Siberian Islands
Lena
Banks Islands
ARCTIC OCEAN
LAPTEV SEA
Victoria Islands
McClure Strait
Nordvik
CANADA
Queen Elizabeth Islands
NORTH MAGNETIC POLE
Severnaya Zemlya
Ellesmere Island
★ NORTH POLE
Dikson
Yenisey
Foxe Basin
Franz Josef Land
LINCOLN SEA
Baffin Island
Novaya Zemlya
BAFFIN BAY
KARA SEA
Ob
Svalbard (Norway)
BARENTS SEA
Davis Strait
GREENLAND (DENMARK)
GREENLAND SEA
Pechora
North Cape
• Murmansk
• Nuuk
• Archangel
NORWEGIAN SEA
ICELAND
• Reykjavik
RUSSIA

ANIMALS OF THE ARCTIC

HARP SEAL PUPS

Prey of Hunters

When they are young, harp seals have soft, white fur. The numbers of seals have dropped because the pups are hunted for this fur.

NORTH AMERICAN CARIBOU

Grazing in the Tundra

Caribou are North American deer. They spend the summer grazing on mosses, grasses, and lichens in the Arctic tundra.

Tundra

The mainland areas in the Arctic Circle are covered with a treeless wilderness called the tundra. The most common animals are caribou and reindeer, but bears, foxes, hares, lemmings, and voles are also found here.

Drying White Fish

Although many Arctic people live in settlements today, traditionally they caught different types of fish and hunted seals for food. Fish that was not eaten immediately was hung up to dry and eaten later.

Icebound Ships

The Arctic ice makes shipping conditions difficult. Over the years, ships, including cruise liners and **expeditions**, have all become stuck in the thick ice.

Animal Adaptation

There are several animals found in the Arctic region, including walruses, Polar bears, arctic foxes, and birds such as snowy owls. Plants and animals that live in the Arctic have **adaptations** to help them survive and raise young in the extreme cold and windy conditions. For example, some plants found in the tundra have furry or waxlike coatings to protect them against the cold and wind.

Walrus

A thick layer of special fat, called blubber, keeps walruses warm.

Polar bear

Paw pads with rough surfaces stop Polar bears from slipping on the ice.

Arctic fox

An extremely thick, long fur coat keeps the Arctic fox warm.

Snowy owl

The snowy owl has feathers on its legs and feet to provide warmth.

CLIMATE

The Earth's climate is a constantly changing system. It is driven by the energy of the Sun. There are five subsystems to our climate: the atmosphere, the biosphere, the hydrosphere, the cryosphere, and the lithosphere. The interactions between these subsystems create different climate zones where the temperature, wind, and rain are all similar.

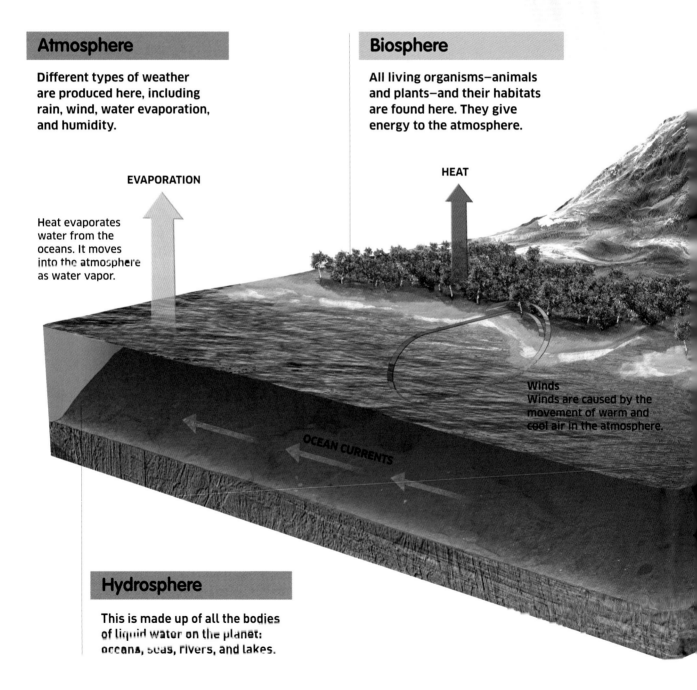

Rain
Water vapor in the atmosphere condenses to form clouds. When the clouds become heavy enough, the water falls as rain or snow.

Atmosphere

Different types of weather are produced here, including rain, wind, water evaporation, and humidity.

Biosphere

All living organisms—animals and plants—and their habitats are found here. They give energy to the atmosphere.

EVAPORATION

Heat evaporates water from the oceans. It moves into the atmosphere as water vapor.

HEAT

Winds
Winds are caused by the movement of warm and cool air in the atmosphere.

OCEAN CURRENTS

Hydrosphere

This is made up of all the bodies of liquid water on the planet: oceans, seas, rivers, and lakes.

59 °F
The average temperature at the Earth's surface.

SOLAR RAYS

The Sun
The Sun provides energy and drives the changes in each subsystem.

Lithosphere

The lithosphere is the outer layer of the Earth, formed of the continents and the ocean floor. Continuous changes to its surface affect the climate.

Cryosphere

The cryosphere is the parts of the planet that are covered in ice or where the rock or soil is below 32 °F. It reflects almost all of the Sun's rays back into the atmosphere.

HEAT

HUMAN ACTIVITY

VOLCANOES
The particles that volcanoes put into the atmosphere block out sunlight and lower temperatures.

Under the volcano
Here, there is molten rock at temperatures of more than 2012 °F.

Return to the sea
Water seeps into the lithosphere and drains through it into the oceans, or the hydrosphere.

FLORA AND FAUNA

The Earth is divided into different biomes. A biome is an area with a particular climate in which the plants and animals that live there are adapted to the conditions. Different biomes include grassland, tundra, and desert. Factors such as the quality of the soil, altitude, and human activity can affect how each species lives within each biome.

Polar bears
When ice forms over the ocean, Polar bears move onto the ice to hunt.

Climate

The Earth's biomes are divided according to the climate in which they are found. Climatic conditions such as wind, temperature, and rainfall determine which organisms live in each biome. Some plants and animals have developed specifically to survive in a certain biome. However, some animals are forced to **migrate** to different biomes with better living conditions.

Distribution
Plants and animals need water to survive. Fewer species are found in habitats where there is less water. These are the world's deserts.

POLAR ZONE

Tundra

SUBPOLAR ZONE

Taiga

HUMANS
Human activity, such as deforestation, has affected many species-rich regions.

TEMPERATE ZONE

TROPICAL ZONE

Desert   Steppe   Grassland   Forest

Desert   Savanna   Forest

Animal Adaptation

Animals have adapted to live in certain biomes. These adaptations ensure their survival. However, when human activity causes changes to their natural habitats, animals find that they have smaller and smaller regions in which to live.

Deserts
Many of the animals that live in deserts, such as the spiny lizard (above), can survive for days on very little food or water.

Polar Regions
Very few species are found in the icy Polar regions. Polar bears (above) have a special thick coat to protect them from the cold.

Marine Biodiversity
There is a wide variety of species in the world's oceans and seas. Large numbers of species are found in the world's warm tropical waters.

Tropical Forests
The tropical forests are home to many different species. This tree frog feeds on crickets, flies, and moths.

Biomes of the World
This map shows the different biomes found on land and in the water.

- Mountains
- Desert
- Grassland
- Taiga
- Temperate forests
- Tropical rain forests
- Polar
- Coral reefs

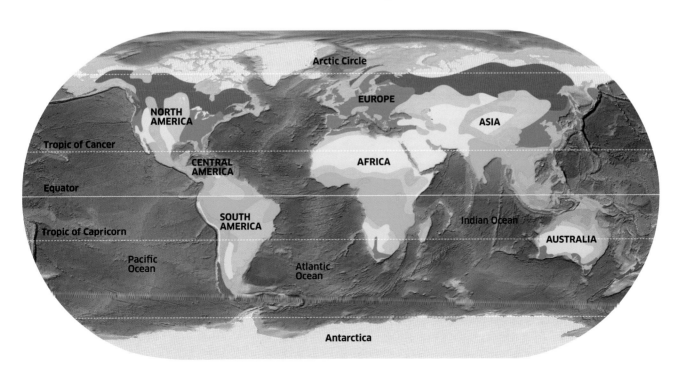

ANTARCTICA

The Antarctic lies south of the Antarctic Circle. It includes most of the world's fifth-largest continent, Antarctica, in the middle of which is the South Pole. Only the tip of the Antarctic Peninsula, jutting out toward South America, lies outside the Antarctic Circle. The waters around Antarctica are called the Southern Ocean or Antarctic Ocean.

INTERNATIONAL PARK?
Many people would like to make Antarctica a protected area, keeping it safe from development.

Antarctic Circle

Ice covers about 98 percent of Antarctica. The average thickness of the ice is 7218 feet, but in places it is 15,748 feet thick. The region is so cold that there are few plants and animals that can survive the icy temperatures. However, the region is home to penguins. These flightless birds feed mainly on the fish they find in the waters around the continent.

Exploring the Antarctic

Early explorers in Antarctica faced great hardship. An expedition first reached the South Pole in 1911. It was led by the Norwegian Roald Amundsen. A British expedition led by Robert Falcon Scott reached the South Pole five weeks later, but Scott and all his team died on the way back.

Map labels: S. Orkney Is., C. Norvegia, Queen Maud Land, S. Shetland Is., WEDDELL SEA, Coats Land, Enderby Land, Antarctic Peninsula, Palmer Archipelago, Mac Robertson Land, CAPE DARNLEY, Berkner Is., Alexander Is., RONNE ICE SHELF, PENSACOLA MTNS., PR. CHARLES MTNS., AMERICAN HIGHLAND, Charcot Is., BELLINGHAUSEN SEA, Palmer Land, Vinson Massif 16,050, SOUTH POLE, GREATER ANTARCTICA, Queen Mary Land, Ellsworth Land, LESSER ANTARCTICA, TRANSANTARCTIC MTNS., Knox Coast, Thurston Is., AMUNDSEN SEA, Mt. Kirkpatric 14,855, Mary Byrd Land, ROSS ICE SHELF, Victoria Land, Wilkes Land, Siple Is., Roosevelt Is., Mt. Erebus 12,448, ROSS SEA, George V Land, C. Adare, SOUTH MAGNETIC POLE

-128.6 °F

The coldest temperature ever recorded was at the Russian Vostok Station.

Roald Amundsen
In 1911, Amundsen was the first man to reach the South Pole. In 1926, he took part in an expedition that flew over the North Pole. He disappeared in June 1928 while on a rescue mission.

Whopping whale
Blue whales, the largest living animals, feed on krill found in the seas around Antarctica.

Trawling Near Antarctica

The cold waters around Antarctica are rich in marine life, including krill (tiny, shrimplike creatures), squid, seals, fish, and whales. An abundance of fish means the area has excellent trawling conditions.

Tents in the Snow

Scientists exploring Antarctica use specially-designed tents called "Scott's Polar Tents," which are very durable and keep in the heat.

Penguin Parade

Adélie penguins, the most common penguins in Antarctica, build nests of pebbles on the coast.

Wandering albatross

Found around the Southern Ocean, these birds feed mainly on squid, fish, and krill. They have the widest wingspan of any living bird at 12 feet.

RESEARCH AND EXPLORATION

OZONE LAYER HOLES

Blocking Harmful Rays

The **ozone layer** in the Earth's upper atmosphere blocks most of the Sun's ultraviolet rays. Pollution has created holes in the ozone layer over Antarctica. Research is being done to discover how this affects the region.

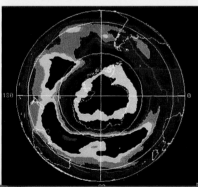

SCIENTISTS IN ANTARCTICA

Vital Supplies

There are several research centers in Antarctica. Some have scientists working there all year round, while others are used just in the summer months. Every day, supplies for these scientists are flown or shipped in to Antarctica.

Ice Cave

Around the coast of Antarctica, the sea hollows out spectacular caves in the ice.

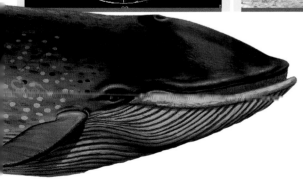

Weather Balloons

Balloons sent up into the atmosphere are used to study weather conditions. The balloons sent up in Antarctica are important because conditions there affect the world's weather.

POPULATION

In 2011, the number of people in the world (the world's population) exceeded 7 billion. However, these people are not spread across the planet evenly. Some areas, such as parts of China, India, and Europe, are densely populated, while other regions, such as Australia and Greenland, have far fewer people living in them.

HUNGER
According to the United Nations, 925 million people in the world do not have enough to eat.

THE 20 MOST-POPULOUS COUNTRIES

1 China 1,343,239,923
2 India 1,205,073,612
3 United States of America 313,847,465
4 Indonesia 248,216,193
5 Brazil 205,716,890
6 Pakistan 190,291,129
7 Nigeria 170,123,740
8 Bangladesh 161,083,804
9 Russia 138,082,178
10 Japan 127,368,088
11 Mexico 114,975,406
12 Philippines 103,775,002
13 Ethiopia 93,815,992
14 Vietnam 91,519,289
15 Egypt 83,688,164
16 Germany 81,305,856
17 Turkey 79,749,461
18 Iran 78,868,711
19 Dem. Republic of Congo 73,599,190
20 Thailand 67,091,089

Population Density

A country's population density is the average number of people living on each square mile of land.

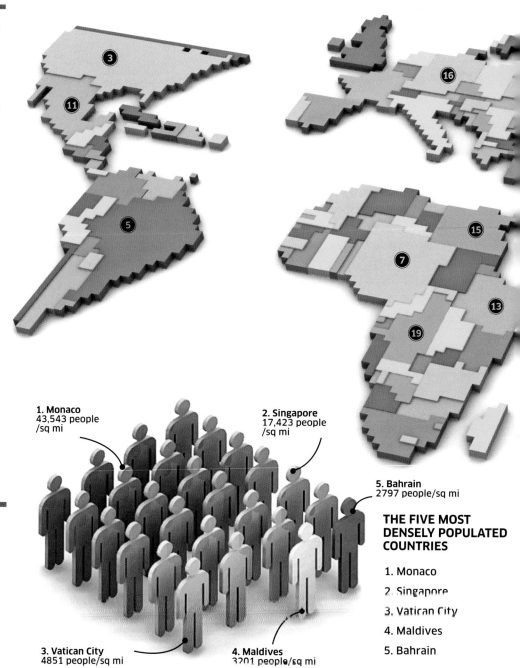

1. Monaco
43,543 people /sq mi

2. Singapore
17,423 people /sq mi

5. Bahrain
2797 people/sq mi

3. Vatican City
4851 people/sq mi

4. Maldives
3201 people/sq mi

THE FIVE MOST DENSELY POPULATED COUNTRIES

1. Monaco
2. Singapore
3. Vatican City
4. Maldives
5. Bahrain

CASE STUDIES
CITY AND COUNTRY

Migration

Migration is the word used for the movement of people from one place to another, both within the same country or from one country to another. People may move in search of work or to leave a war-torn area.

Urbanization

People often migrate from the countryside to live in cities or towns. This is called **urbanization**. Trinidad and Tobago in the Caribbean has a very low level of urbanization. Just 13 percent of people live in cities or towns.

40%

The predicted increase in world population by 2050, according to the United Nations.

THE THREE MAIN RELIGIONS IN THE WORLD

1. Christianity
2.1 billion followers

2. Islam
1.5 billion followers

3. Hinduism
900 million followers

POPULATION GROWTH 2000–2010

The world's population is growing fastest in less economically developed areas. Many rich parts of the world are already very densely populated.

Population growth 2000–2010:
- África: 26.1%
- Australia: 15%
- South America: 13.2%
- Asia: 12.7%
- North America: 10.4%
- Europe: 0.8%

THE MODERN WORLD

In recent centuries, human activity has been changing the planet. Large areas of forest have been cut down to make way for farms, while pollution from industry is harming the atmosphere. This is having a serious effect on the environment, and in coming years, we will need to find new ways to live that are less harmful to the planet we depend on.

CARBON
The level of **carbon dioxide** in the atmosphere has increased by 40 percent in the last 150 years.

❶
NEOLITHIC
Humans first started to farm about 10,000 years ago. The farmers built towns to live in and for the first time, people settled in one place rather than moving around as nomads.

❸
INDUSTRIAL AGE
The Industrial Age saw more people living in cities and more manufacturing. The manufacturing caused an increase in pollution.

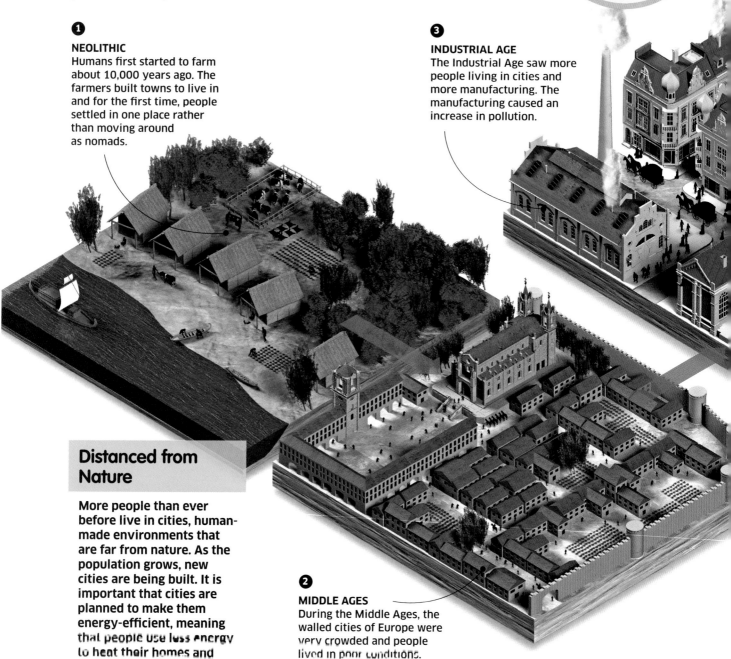

Distanced from Nature

More people than ever before live in cities, human-made environments that are far from nature. As the population grows, new cities are being built. It is important that cities are planned to make them energy-efficient, meaning that people use less energy to heat their homes and travel to work.

❷
MIDDLE AGES
During the Middle Ages, the walled cities of Europe were very crowded and people lived in poor conditions.

7 billion

The world's population in 2011. A thousand years ago, there were only 300 million people, the population of the United States today.

400 million

The estimated number of dogs in the world.

22,000

The number of Polar bears in the world.

❹

21ST CENTURY
Humans begin to find ways to cut down on pollution and to live in less destructive ways.

Overpopulation

The increased number of people in the world is putting a huge strain on the environment. New forms of development that do not destroy the environment are needed. This is called sustainable development.

Threats
Overpopulation is the root of many problems, including hunger, climate change, pollution, and the destruction of wildlife.

CLIMATE CHANGE

In recent years, the average temperature of the Earth has been slowly rising. This increase in average temperature is called global warming. The main cause of global warming is human activity. While the change in temperature both on land and in the sea has been gradual, global warming is changing the world's climate, which is causing serious problems in some parts of the world.

CORAL REEFS
Many coral reefs are dying because of the increase in sea temperature.

THE EFFECTS OF GLOBAL WARMING

The global temperature has increased by a few tenths of a degree in the last few decades. Although this seems like a small change, life on the Earth is delicately balanced, and a small change in temperature can have a serious effect. Global warming has become a major threat to the welfare of all living beings.

50%

The reduction in population of Adélie penguins because of ice loss in Antarctica in the last 30 years.

Thawing at the Poles
The rise in temperature is causing large amounts of ice at the Polar caps to melt. This leads to an increase in sea level.

Floods
Climate change is causing large floods. In recent years, Bangladesh has seen some of the worst floods in its history.

Islands Under the Water
The small Pacific islands of Tuvalu and Kiribati and the Maldives in the Indian Ocean are very low-lying, which makes them vulnerable to rising sea levels. If the oceans rise just several feet, this will leave the islands completely underwater.

Disappearing glaciers
As a result of global warming, many glaciers in mountainous regions are shrinking.

Desertification
Climate change is causing drought in central Asia. This leads to poor harvests and a shortage of food.

Greenhouse Effect

Greenhouses are specially built to trap heat so that plants can be grown. Similarly, the greenhouse effect is a natural process where the gases in the Earth's atmosphere trap some of the Sun's energy. Without the greenhouse effect, the planet would be too cold to live on.

Carbon dioxide and methane are both greenhouse gases. Carbon dioxide is given off when coal, gas, and oil are burned. Methane is given off by cattle. Increases in the level of both of these gases in the atmosphere means that the average temperature of the Earth is increasing.

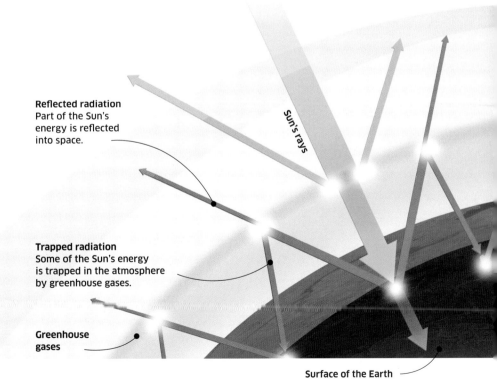

Reflected radiation
Part of the Sun's energy is reflected into space.

Sun's rays

Trapped radiation
Some of the Sun's energy is trapped in the atmosphere by greenhouse gases.

Greenhouse gases

Surface of the Earth

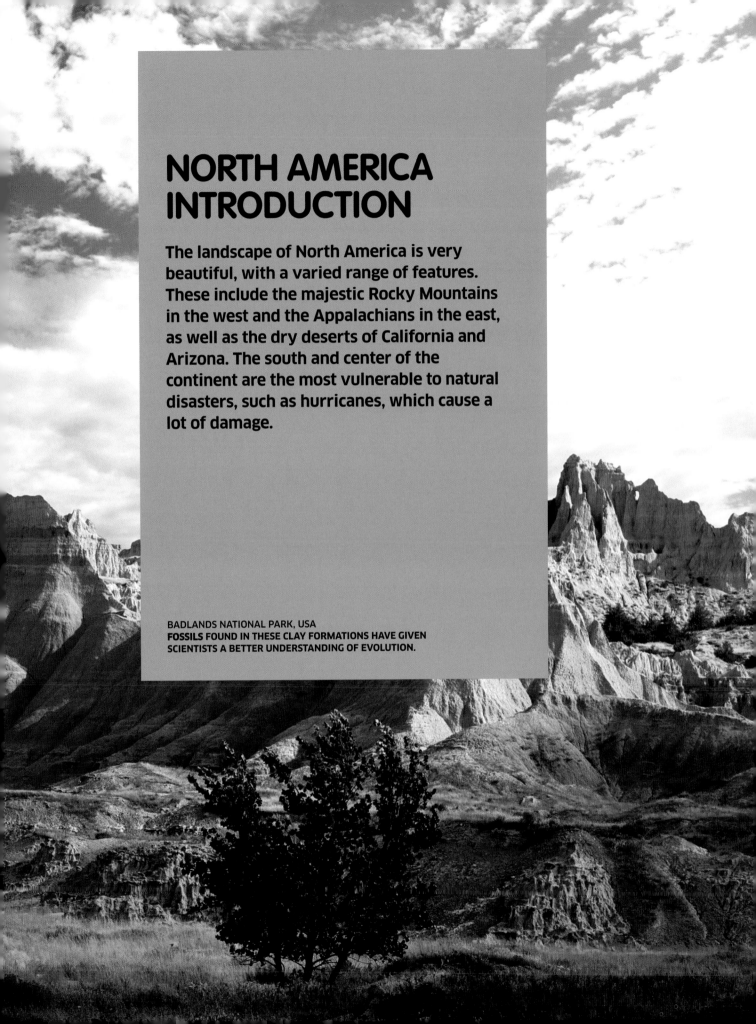

NORTH AMERICA INTRODUCTION

The landscape of North America is very beautiful, with a varied range of features. These include the majestic Rocky Mountains in the west and the Appalachians in the east, as well as the dry deserts of California and Arizona. The south and center of the continent are the most vulnerable to natural disasters, such as hurricanes, which cause a lot of damage.

BADLANDS NATIONAL PARK, USA
FOSSILS FOUND IN THESE CLAY FORMATIONS HAVE GIVEN SCIENTISTS A BETTER UNDERSTANDING OF EVOLUTION.

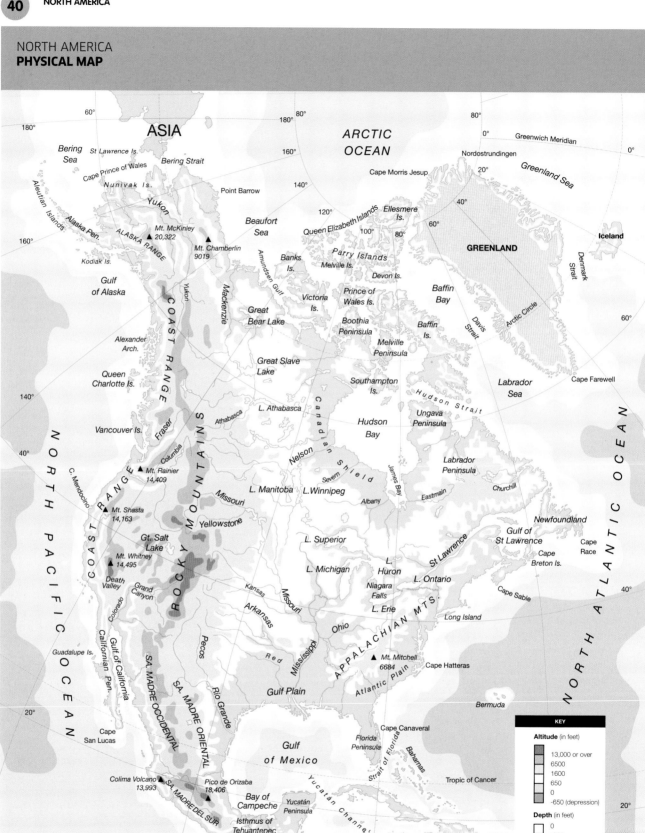

ASIA

Bering
Sea

St Lawrence Is.

Cape Prince of Wales

Bering Strait

Nunivak Is.

Yukon

ALASKA RANGE

▲ Mt. McKinley
20,322

▲ Mt. Chamberlin
9019

Point Barrow

ARCTIC
OCEAN

Greenwich Meridian

Nordostrundingen

Greenland Sea

Cape Morris Jesup

Beaufort
Sea

Queen Elizabeth Islands

Ellesmere
Is.

GREENLAND

Iceland

Denmark
Strait

Aleutian Islands

Alaska Pen.

Kodiak Is.

Gulf
of Alaska

Yukon

COAST RANGE

Mackenzie

Amundsen Gulf

Banks
Is.

Parry Islands
Melville Is.

Devon Is.

Victoria
Is.

Prince
of
Wales Is.

Boothia
Peninsula

Baffin
Bay

Baffin
Is.

Davis
Strait

Arctic Circle

Cape Farewell

Alexander
Arch.

Queen
Charlotte Is.

Vancouver Is.

Great
Bear Lake

Great Slave
Lake

Melville
Peninsula

Southampton
Is.

Labrador
Sea

Hudson Strait

Fraser

Athabasca

L. Athabasca

Canadian Shield

Hudson
Bay

Ungava
Peninsula

Columbia

▲ Mt. Rainier
14,409

C. Mendocino

▲ Mt. Shasta
14,163

ROCKY MOUNTAINS

Missouri

Yellowstone

Nelson

Severn

James Bay

Labrador
Peninsula

Albany

Eastmain

Churchill

Newfoundland

NORTH PACIFIC OCEAN

Gt. Salt
Lake

▲ Mt. Whitney
14,495

Death
Valley

Grand
Canyon

Colorado

Kansas

Missouri

L. Manitoba

L. Winnipeg

L. Superior

L. Michigan

L. Huron

Niagara
Falls

L. Ontario

L. Erie

St Lawrence

Gulf of
St Lawrence

Cape
Breton Is.

Cape
Race

Long Island

Guadalupe Is.

Gulf of California

Californian Pen.

SA. MADRE OCCIDENTAL

Pecos

Rio Grande

Arkansas

Red

Mississippi

Ohio

APPALACHIAN MTS.

▲ Mt. Mitchell
6684

Cape Sable

Cape Hatteras

Atlantic Plain

NORTH ATLANTIC OCEAN

Cape
San Lucas

SA. MADRE ORIENTAL

Gulf Plain

Bermuda

Colima Volcano ▲
13,993

SA. MADRE DEL SUR

Pico de Orizaba
18,406 ▲

Bay of
Campeche

Yucatán
Peninsula

Gulf
of Mexico

Isthmus of
Tehuantepec

Florida
Peninsula

Cape Canaveral

Strait of Florida

Bahamas

Tropic of Cancer

Yucatán Channel

Caribbean Sea

KEY		
Altitude (in feet)		
	13,000 or over	
	6500	
	1600	
	650	
	0	
	-650 (depression)	
Depth (in feet)		
	0	
	-650	
	-6500	
	-18,500 or over	

Scale

0   1000 miles

NORTH AMERICA
POLITICAL MAP

ASIA

Bering Sea

St Lawrence Is.

Nunivak Is.

Aleutian Islands

Alaska
(USA)

• Anchorage

Kodiak Is.

Alexander Arch.

Queen Charlotte Is.

ARCTIC OCEAN

Beaufort Sea

Queen Elizabeth Islands

Parry Islands

Banks Is. *Melville Is.*

Devon Is.

Prince of Wales Is.

Victoria Is.

Baffin Bay

Baffin Is.

Southampton Is.

Labrador Sea

Greenwich Meridian

Greenland Sea

GREENLAND
(Denmark)

Arctic Circle **Iceland**

CANADA

Hudson Bay

Vancouver Is. • Edmonton

• Vancouver

Seattle •

• Calgary

Portland •

• Winnipeg

Newfoundland

Cape Breton Is.

UNITED STATES OF AMERICA

• Sacramento

• San Francisco

• Salt Lake City

Minneapolis •

Quebec •

Montreal •

Ottawa ◉

• Los Angeles

Denver •

Milwaukee •

Chicago •

Toronto •

• Buffalo

• Boston

Las Vegas •

Detroit •

• Cleveland

• New York

• San Diego

Kansas City •

Indianapolis •

Columbus •

Pittsburgh •

Tijuana •

• Phoenix

St Louis •

Cincinnati •

• Philadelphia

Washington DC ◉

Guadalupe Is.

El Paso •

Ciudad Juárez •

• Dallas

• Atlanta

San Antonio •

Houston •

Monterrey •

New Orleans •

Bermuda (UK)

MEXICO

Tampa •

• Orlando

Miami •

BAHAMAS
◉ **Nassau**

Guadalajara •

• Querétaro

Gulf of Mexico

Toluca •

Mexico City ◉

• Mérida

Puebla • • Veracruz

Oaxaca de • Juárez

Tropic of Cancer

Caribbean Sea

NORTH PACIFIC OCEAN

NORTH ATLANTIC OCEAN

Scale

0 _____ 1000 miles

180° 60° 180° 80° 160° 140° 120° 100° 80° 0° 20° 40° 60° 20°

160° 140° 40° 20° 60° 40° 20°

100° 80° 60°

THE ROCKY MOUNTAINS

This mountain chain, also known as the Rockies, runs parallel to the west coast of North America, covering over 3000 miles. The mountains sweep down from northwest Canada to the southwestern United States. They are a popular tourist destination, especially for hiking, camping, fishing, mountain biking, skiing, and snowboarding.

VISITS
More than 3 million visitors go to the Rocky Mountain National Park every year.

Four Regions

The Rockies border the Great Plains to the east and the Rocky Mountain Trench to the west. The mountains are sometimes divided into four sections (right). This includes the Brooks Range, which extends from Canada into Alaska, and is often thought of as an extension of the Rockies.

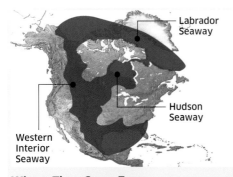

Labrador Seaway

Hudson Seaway

Western Interior Seaway

Where They Came From

The Rockies are young mountains that formed 75 million years ago. They first appeared when the ocean floor emerged out of the sea in a great arch.

Arctic Province
The Alaska Range is home to North America's highest peak, Mount McKinley, which sits at 20,322 ft.

Northern Province
From British Columbia, the Rockies stretch through Canada and continue into the US states of Washington, Idaho, and Wyoming. This part of the chain is extremely rugged and beautiful, with glaciers in some areas. Mount Robson (12,972 ft) is the highest peak in this region.

Central Province
This region includes Wyoming, and its highest peak is Gannett Peak at 13,802 ft.

Southern Province
This area has the highest **elevation** of the Rockies. Its highest peak is Mount Elbert at 14,432 ft.

Profile

This profile of the Southern Province Rockies gives an impression of the majestic peaks of the mountains.

Alaska Range

Brooks Range

Mount McKinley

ALASKA

CANADA

Mount Robson

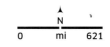
UNITED STATES

Gannett Peak

Mount Elbert

■ The Rockies

N

0   mi   621

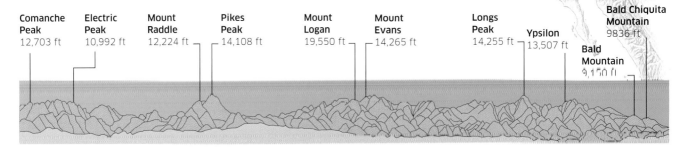

Comanche Peak 12,703 ft	Electric Peak 10,992 ft	Mount Raddle 12,224 ft	Pikes Peak 14,108 ft	Mount Logan 19,550 ft	Mount Evans 14,265 ft	Longs Peak 14,255 ft	Ypsilon 13,507 ft	Bald Chiquita Mountain 9836 ft

Bald Mountain 9,150 ft

THE APPALACHIANS

The most prominent feature of the landscape in eastern North America is the Appalachian mountain range. These fold mountains formed around 480 million years ago. Mount Mitchell is the highest peak, at 6684 feet.

MINING

Mining in this mountain area is threatening wildlife.

Colorful highlands
Small, colorful shrubs cover the highlands of Appalachia.

American Holly

With its bright red berries, American holly is found in the region.

Cottontail Rabbit

The cottontail rabbit is one of the most common inhabitants of the region.

FACT FILE

Mount Mitchell
Located in North Carolina, east of the Mississippi, Mount Mitchell is the highest point of the Appalachians.

Fauna and Flora
The mountains are home to many different plant and animal species. The most common animals found in the mountains include black bears, deer, and elk, as well as numerous insects and rodents.

Susquehanna River
The Susquehanna River runs through the Appalachians. Its source is in New York State and it crosses through Pennsylvania and Maryland.

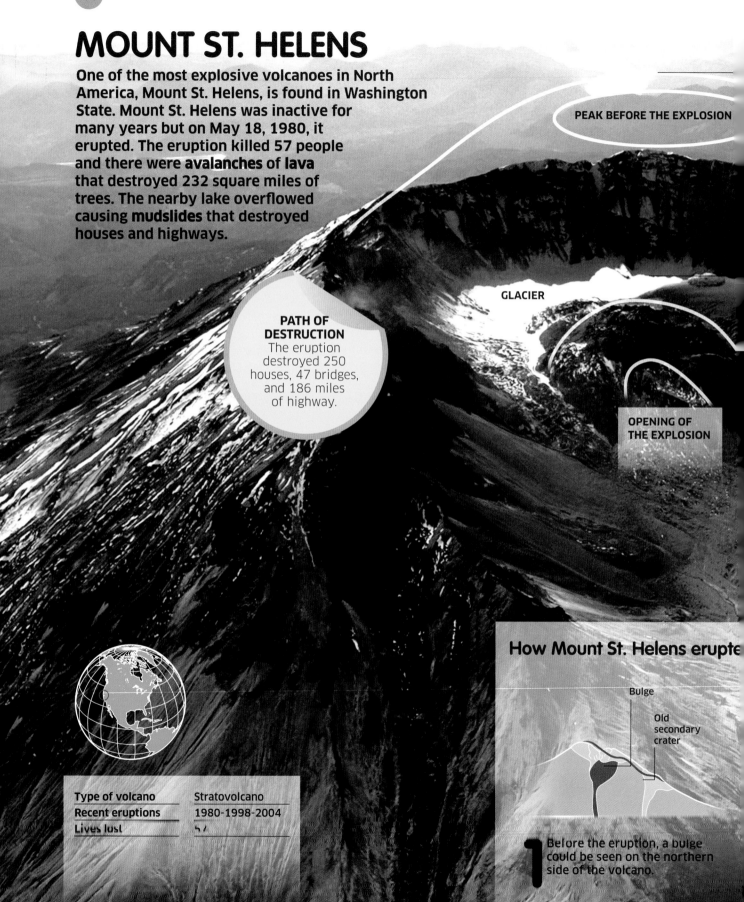

MOUNT ST. HELENS

One of the most explosive volcanoes in North America, Mount St. Helens, is found in Washington State. Mount St. Helens was inactive for many years but on May 18, 1980, it erupted. The eruption killed 57 people and there were **avalanches** of **lava** that destroyed 232 square miles of trees. The nearby lake overflowed causing **mudslides** that destroyed houses and highways.

PEAK BEFORE THE EXPLOSION

GLACIER

PATH OF DESTRUCTION
The eruption destroyed 250 houses, 47 bridges, and 186 miles of highway.

OPENING OF THE EXPLOSION

Type of volcano	Stratovolcano
Recent eruptions	1980-1998-2004
Lives lost	57

How Mount St. Helens erupte

Bulge

Old secondary crater

1 Before the eruption, a bulge could be seen on the northern side of the volcano.

9678 ft

After the eruption,
Mount St. Helens
lost its cone shape.

-1316 ft

8363 ft

THE ERUPTION OF MOUNT ST. HELENS

Before and after the Eruption

Mount St. Helens was a striking feature of the landscape. Before the eruption, forests and fields surrounded the volcano. The eruption left the top of the volcano as a horseshoe-shaped pit, with nothing around it.

During the Explosion

The energy released was many times more powerful than an atomic bomb. The explosion lasted more than nine hours.

Volcanic ash burned trees and destroyed forests for several miles.

Crater is blocked

The magma could not escape and pressure built up on the northern side

The cone became blocked

The crater explodes

The blockages caused an avalanche of magma and ash

A column of smoke and ash rose 12 miles in height

Profile before eruption

Profile after eruption

2 Pressure built up on the northern side.

3 Magma and gases erupted in a huge explosion.

4 The ash eruption appeared at its most powerful.

THE SEMIDESERT HABITAT

Rainfall is rare in the semidesert, but the small amount of precipitation is what makes the difference between this habitat and a desert. The moisture ensures that cactuses, shrubs, and many other plants can grow. The abundance of these plants at certain times of the year, especially in spring and summer, attracts animal species. In winter, it is very cold and dry, and the wildlife hibernates or seeks shelter.

Storing Water

Plants with leaves and thick stems, or roots close to the surface, can absorb moisture easily from the rare rainfalls. The cacti leaves will change to thorns, minimizing the moisture they lose and protecting them from hungry animals.

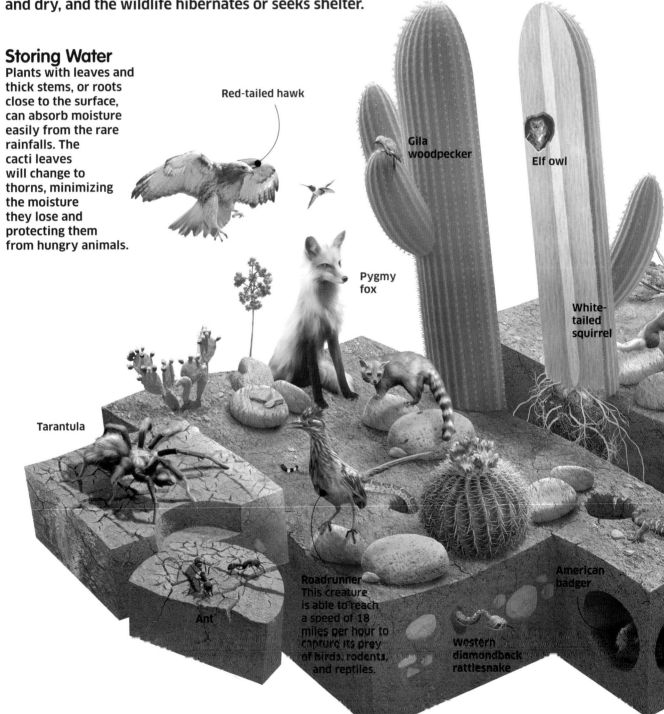

Red-tailed hawk

Gila woodpecker

Elf owl

Pygmy fox

White-tailed squirrel

Tarantula

Ant

Roadrunner
This creature is able to reach a speed of 18 miles per hour to capture its prey of birds, rodents, and reptiles.

Western diamondback rattlesnake

American badger

Saguaro cactus
This cactus's fleshy stem expands like a musical accordion to store water at a volume of 80 percent of its weight. Its stem may reach a height nearly 46 feet, and it can weigh up to 10 tons. Its roots are shallow but can extend up to 98 feet.

The American Semidesert
In winter, the temperature in a semidesert habitat can drop to -22 °F. These harsh conditions cause animals living there to use the vegetation and cactuses as places to shelter. They also provide a source of water.

THE SEMIDESERTS OF NORTH AMERICA

Overview
In the semidesert habitat, only moisture-storing plants, such as cactuses, can survive on the small amount of available moisture. A little more than 8.5 fl oz of rain falls each year.

Plants
Desert plants flourish in this habitat. The ocotillo (below) sheds its leaves once it has absorbed enough moisture to survive, leaving thorns to protect it.

Coyote

Musk hog

Black-tailed jackrabbit

Desert tortoise

Gila monster

Wildlife
An adult desert tortoise (below) can survive without water for almost a year. Its front legs are specially adapted to dig large, deep burrows, from which it comes out to feed in the morning and evening. It can live for between 50 and 80 years.

Desert scorpion
This creature has a weapon in its tail that injects venom into its prey.

OIL EXPLOSION

On April 20, 2010, BP's oil rig Deepwater Horizon exploded in the Gulf of Mexico, 43.5 miles off the coast of New Orleans, and sank two days later. Until the well was sealed in September, thousands of gallons of oil spilled into the ocean each day, having a devastating effect on the environment.

Oil Spill
US officials were quick to establish barriers in order to prevent the spill reaching the coast.

DISPERSANTS OF OIL

How They Work
Chemical dispersants are used to help clean up oil spills. They quickly break the oil down into natural substances.

The dispersant, which contains cleaning chemicals, is applied.

The chemicals get into the oil.

The chemicals reduce the surface tension of the oil.

Oil droplets start to emerge from the layer.

A shiny coat is left once the oil has been broken down.

TEAMWORK
CLEANING THE COAST

The Battle
The success of cleaning up an oil spill depends largely on good organization and teamwork. Sometimes, the oil can be contained using sandbags (right).

Cleaners
To remove oil from coastal rocks, high-pressure washers can be used (right).

Ecological Disaster
The Deepwater Horizon extracted oil from the seabed.

OIL SPILL
NATURAL DISASTER

Fisheries Closed

In Louisiana, oysters and shrimp had to be thrown away because they were exposed to oil (below).

Special Volunteers

Volunteers helped to clean the feathers of pelicans found off the coast of Louisiana.

Environmental Awareness

Environmentalists around the world protested (below) to express their anger over the Gulf of Mexico spill.

Long-Term Poison

The oil spill has harmed deep-water species, such as sea turtles (below), which migrate to the Mexican coast.

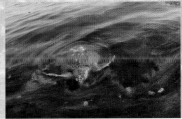

CLIMATE

The North American climate can be extreme and very varied—from the icy temperatures of Alaska, to the dry heat of the deserts of Mexico and the southwestern United States. There are also frequent hurricanes and tornadoes.

Hurricane Katrina
Severe floods followed the New Orleans hurricane in 2005.

HURRICANE KATRINA

In the Gulf of Mexico

Starting in the Gulf of Mexico in August 2005, Hurricane Katrina was one of the most powerful **tropical storms** to hit the USA.

Flooding in New Orleans

The strong winds caused by Katrina flooded New Orleans and submerged much of the city (below).

TORNADOES
TEXAS

Swirling Air

Tornadoes are common in the state of Texas. They appear as a column of hot air destroying everything in their path.

THUNDER AND LIGHTNING
GULF OF MEXICO

Moisture and Heat

The Gulf of Mexico causes an excess of heat and moisture in its atmosphere. When hot air collides with cold air, thunderstorms form.

WEATHER ALERT
UNITED STATES

Traffic Chaos

When there is an extreme weather alert, people are told to leave their homes and to travel to a place of safety. This causes traffic problems.

Anza-Borrego State Park
This park in the Californian desert is home to plants that can tolerate drought.

Coyote

The coyote is a skillful hunter perfectly adapted to the desert environment.

Snakes

Poisonous rattlesnakes are found in the desert areas of the United States.

DESERTS
UNITED STATES

Red Rock Canyon Park
Wind and rain have been eroding the landscape of Red Rock Park for some time (below). The striking formations have been used as the backdrop for many movies.

Chihuahuan Desert
One of the largest deserts in North America is the Chihuahaun (below). Its temperatures are extreme with low temperatures in the winter and very hot summers.

Cozumel, Mexico
The island of Cozumel is located 11 miles off the coast of Yucatan. Ocean currents in the Gulf of Mexico cause mild temperatures of about 79 °F, making it a popular tourist destination. It is home to several unique animal species, including the dwarf raccoon.

POPULATION AND ECONOMY

According to the Census Bureau of the United States, the total population in 2012 was 313,136,227, and its population growth is among the highest in **industrialized** countries. Canada and the United States are highly industrialized countries and are considered global powers.

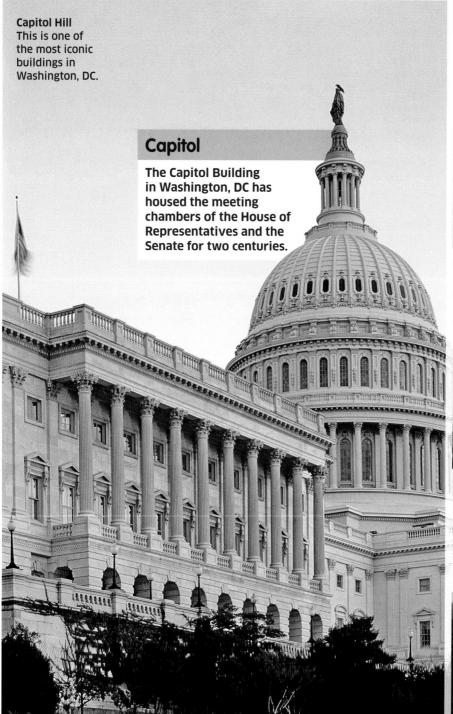

Capitol Hill
This is one of the most iconic buildings in Washington, DC.

Capitol

The Capitol Building in Washington, DC has housed the meeting chambers of the House of Representatives and the Senate for two centuries.

UNITED STATES
HUMAN GEOGRAPHY

Miami, Florida

Miami (below) is one of the most densely populated cities in the United States, along with New York City.

Cape Canaveral

Cape Canaveral is the main center for US space activities. It is located on the Atlantic coast of Florida.

Silicon Valley, California

High-tech industries have flourished in Silicon Valley, California. The area includes the Santa Clara Valley and the southern half of the San Francisco Peninsula.

Palace of Fine Arts
Located in the historic center of Mexico City.

Aerial View

Mexico City is the largest city in Mexico, with more than 20 million people. It is divided into different neighborhoods or districts, each with its own unique features.

ECONOMY
CANADA

Industry

Canada is one of the world's most economically developed countries. Computer industries, automotives, electronics, aeronautics, and chemicals are very important to the economy. Forests of spruce, pine, and cedar allow the large-scale manufacturing of paper pulp and newsprint.

Nathan Phillips Square
This plaza is at the heart of downtown Toronto, Canada.

MEXICO CITY

Although it is crowded and has a high level of pollution, Mexico City is steeped in history. The historic center is built on the ruins of the Aztec capital, and in the elegant district of the Reformation, colonial architecture sits alongside modern buildings.

Country	Mexico
Area	573 sq mi
Population	8,840,000 (city proper)
Density	15,416 people per sq m

EMBLEM OF THE CITY

The Angel of Independence

The Angel of Independence was built to honor those who fought against Spanish rule. It was erected in 1910 and was designed by Antonio Rivas Mercado. The monument is located in the Paseo de la Reforma avenue, which connects the center of the city with Chapultepec.

The Winged Victory
The bronze statue (right and below) shows an angel in flight with open arms. In her right hand she holds a wreath.

Burritos
Typical Mexican food includes burritos. Filled with meat and vegetables, these tortilla wraps (below) are served with spicy sauces.

The Cathedral

This is the largest cathedral in Latin America and dominates the main square of Mexico City. The church and its chapels are ornately decorated.

The Zócalo
A view of the main square.

Women's Collective

Buses used exclusively by women and children (left) run along the main city streets. There are also different subway lines, buses, and trains.

Frida Kahlo Museum

The artist Frida Kahlo lived and died in the neighborhood of Coyoacan. Today, this house (left) is a museum that exhibits many of her personal items, such as her bed and dresses.

National Palace

The National Palace is an important government building in Mexico. The staircase walls and two courtyard walls are decorated with colorful murals by the Mexican painter Diego Rivera.

THE CITY SQUARE

The Zócalo is one of the largest squares in the world. Flags fly in its center and on public buildings, restaurants, and hotels.

PARKS AND PROMENADES
CHAPULTEPEC AND XOCHIMILCO

Restful Places in a Busy City

Xochimilco (below) is the only place in Mexico City that still houses the floating gardens (or chinampas), built by the Aztecs.

Chapultepec Park is an enormous green area (bottom) in the middle of this bustling city.

Population

Mexico's constitution recognizes 62 different groups of peoples in the country who have strong links with this region throughout history. This ensures that their culture and language are protected.

THE STATUE OF LIBERTY

One of the world's most famous monuments stands on Liberty Island, south of Manhattan, in New York City. The monument is called "Liberty Enlightening the World" and was a gift from France to the United States in 1886.

TECHNICAL DESCRIPTION

Opened:
October 28, 1886

Location:
Liberty Island,
New York

Construction:
The figure is made from copper plates. Due to the size and weight of the stone base, it rests on four gigantic steel supports.

IN DETAIL

Support
The statue's strength is created by an internal tower. A skeleton around this tower keeps the outer layer of copper in place.

Plaque
Inside the statue is a plaque with the poem "The New Colossus" by Emma Lazarus.

Base
The base is square and rests on a star-shaped plinth.

Museums
There are two museums at the foot of the statue.

Head
To reach the head, visitors must climb 354 steps. It is 16 feet from the chin to the skull.

The Sculptor

The statue is the work of the French sculptor Frédéric Auguste Bartholdi. An ancient statue, the Colossus of Rhodes, inspired him.

Torch
The torch was originally made from copper, but in 1916, it was changed to 600 pieces of yellow glass to enhance its brightness. The flame is covered with gold leaf.

Manhattan
The statue gives tourists some of the best views of Manhattan Island. With a population of just over 8.1 million, Manhattan is considered one of the largest urban areas in the world.

Crown
There are seven points in the statue's crown. They symbolize the seven seas and the seven continents of the world.

Elevator

An elevator goes as far as the 10th floor. The 12 further floors must be reached by foot.

Tablet
There is a tablet in the left hand that bears the date of US Independence.

328 ft

The height of the statue from the base to the torch.

Vision
The statue was the first thing **immigrants** saw when they arrived by boat in the United States.

Statue
Close-up view of the famous monument.

CENTRAL AMERICA AND THE CARIBBEAN INTRODUCTION

Central America and the Caribbean separate North and South America. The region has areas of volcanic activity as well as places of great natural beauty. The warm tropical climate produces lush vegetation, such as rain forests. The warm, clear waters of the Atlantic Ocean and the Caribbean Sea are home to beautiful coral reefs.

INCREDIBLE HABITAT
THE BELIZE RAIN FOREST IS HOME TO THOUSANDS OF SPECIES OF ANIMALS AND PLANTS.

FLORA AND FAUNA

Mountains, sea-washed shores, and tropical rain forests
are found throughout Central America and the Caribbean.
The region's plants and animals are very varied.
Alligators, iguanas, and coral reefs are all found here.

Kinkajou

The kinkajou, also
known as the honey
bear, lives in Central
America. It is a
nocturnal mammal
that lives in trees
and feeds on fruits.

Jaguar

The jaguar (left) is the
largest carnivore in the
Americas and one of the
largest worldwide. This cat
is in danger of **extinction**.

Macaw

The red-and-green
macaw (left) nests in
hollow trees in the
region's forests. It feeds
on seeds and fruit.

Quetzal

With its brightly colored feathers and long tail, the quetzal is the national bird of Guatemala.

Reptiles

The green iguana lives in areas of thick vegetation where there is an average annual temperature of 82 °F.

Guatemala Semuc Champey is a beautiful lake on the Cahabón River in Guatemala.

Silvertip Shark

The silvertip shark is found in the Pacific Ocean. It reaches a maximum length of 10 feet. It is a danger to humans.

NATURE RESERVE
TIKAL NATIONAL PARK

Forest Ruins

The Tikal National Park is found in the Petén region of Guatemala. The park is home to pumas, jaguars, birds such as toucans, and parrots, and many species of monkey. Tikal was once one of the biggest cities of the Mayan civilization. The ruins of the city lie in the park.

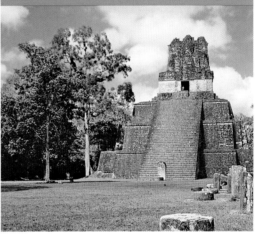

COLORFUL MARINE LIFE

Coral Reefs in Belize

Beautiful coral reefs lie just off the shore of Belize. The reefs are about 186 miles long. They are the second largest in the world, after the Great Barrier Reef in Australia. These reefs are home to many different species of fish.

POPULATION AND ECONOMY

Much of the population of Central America and the Caribbean descend from Africans, Europeans, and Asians. The economies of most of the countries are based on tourism and agriculture. Bananas, cotton, sugar cane, and tobacco are some of the most widely-grown crops.

Haití
Street vendors in Haiti sell fruit and vegetables.

Bananas
Many different fruits are grown for export. There is a high demand for bananas exported from the region.

Tobacco
One of the world's most valuable crops, tobacco is grown in Cuba, Guatemala, Nicaragua, the Dominican Republic, and Honduras.

Sugar Cane
The region produces large amounts of sugar cane. It is usually harvested by hand, providing work for many people.

MAIN
ETHNIC GROUPS

African Heritage

African influences can be seen in many aspects of daily life in the region. For example, there is music that has developed from African traditions, such as the mambo. Many of the people also hold spiritual beliefs that are based on African religions.

Dominican Republic
This is a typical fishing village located on the northwest coast.

Junkanoo
On this holiday in the Bahamas, the biggest parade takes place in Nassau.

EVERYDAY LIFE
GENDER ROLES

Role of Women

In this region, women often have to work harder than men. Recent studies confirm that women spend more time in unpaid activities than men.

LOSS OF CROPS
HEAVY RAINS

Honduras

In 2010, heavy rains fell across Honduras. This caused landslides that destroyed many homes and ruined many of the crops.

THE PANAMA CANAL

A work of engineering brilliance, the Panama Canal allows ships to move between the Atlantic and Pacific oceans without going around South America. The first ship passed through the canal in 1914. In 2007, building began on an extension of the canal.

LAKE

CHAMBER

Ocean to Ocean

It is 50 miles from one ocean to the other, traveling through the Panama Canal.

CHAMBER

There and Back
There are two parallel channels, one for raising the water level and the other for lowering it.

CHAMBER

The Lake
At the center of the canal is a lake, which is 85 feet above sea level. Its water fills the locks.

CHAMBER

Building Works

Currently, 14,000 ships cross the canal each year. Once the building works are completed, 18,000 ships will pass through the canal.

How the Locks Work

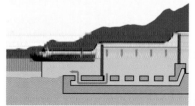

❶ The water in the first lock chamber must be at sea level. To reach sea level, it releases 100 million gallons of fresh water in just eight minutes.

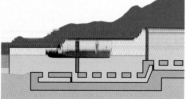

❷ When its water is at sea level, the ship enters the first chamber. The valves and dampers are then closed, and the water is returned to the lock to raise the water level.

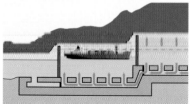

❸ Water flows out of the second chamber to lower its level to the same as the first chamber. The ship passes into the second chamber, and the process is repeated for the third chamber.

8–10 hours

The average time taken to travel through the canal by boat.

THE NEW CANAL
WORK BEGAN IN 2007

Large Ships

For decades, most of the world's **cargo** was carried on ships that were specifically built to travel through the canal. However, many of today's ships are now too large to pass through the canal.

Giant Locks

Two new locks (positioned next to the current canal) will make it possible for these larger ships to travel through the canal. The new canal will also have a system of pools to save fresh water.

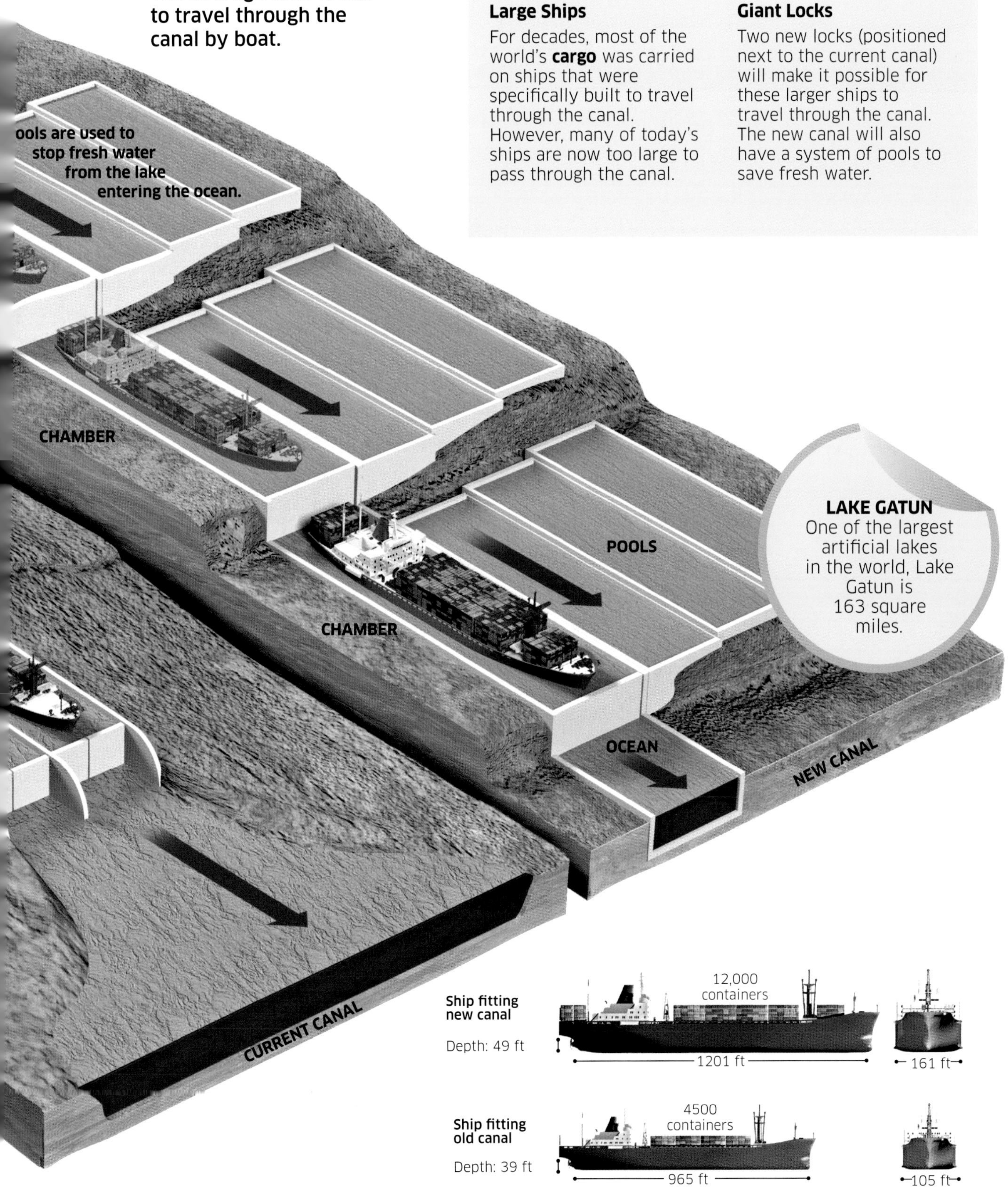

ools are used to stop fresh water from the lake entering the ocean.

CHAMBER

CHAMBER

POOLS

OCEAN

NEW CANAL

LAKE GATUN
One of the largest artificial lakes in the world, Lake Gatun is 163 square miles.

CURRENT CANAL

Ship fitting new canal

Depth: 49 ft

12,000 containers

1201 ft

161 ft

Ship fitting old canal

Depth: 39 ft

4500 containers

965 ft

105 ft

SOUTH AMERICA INTRODUCTION

This large continent extends from the northern hemisphere down close to the Antarctic Circle. It has a huge range of climates, from tropical rain forest and hot desert, to the dry cold of Patagonia in southern Argentina. Most of the continent forms part of an area called Latin America, which is made up of the former colonies of Spain and Portugal. For this reason, Spanish and Portuguese are the most widely spoken languages. There are also a large number of other languages and cultures on the continent. In the Amazon Rain Forest, there are still a few small groups of people who have never contacted the outside world.

THICK CLOUDS
THE ANDES MOUNTAINS RUN ALONG THE WEST OF THE CONTINENT, PARALLEL TO THE PACIFIC COAST.

SOUTH AMERICA
PHYSICAL MAP

Caribbean Sea

NORTH
PACIFIC
OCEAN

NORTH
ATLANTIC
OCEAN

G. of Venezuela
Guajira
Peninsula
Lesser Antilles
Margarita Is.
Trinidad
Panama
Canal
L. Maracaibo
CORD. DE MERIDA
Orinoco Delta
Orinoco Plains
Orinoco
Angel Falls
GUIANA SHIELD
Cape Grande
PACARAIMA MTS.
G. of Panama
Nevado del Tolima 17,110
CORD. OCCIDENTAL
CORD. ORIENTAL
Punta Galera
Pico da Neblina 9990
Negro
Branco
Amazon Estuary
Punta Negra
Equator
0°
Galápagos Is.
Cotopaxi 19,347
Chimborazo 20,561
Japurá
Juruá
Tocantins
Gulf of Guayaquil
Sechura Desert
Ucayali
Amazon Basin
Amazon
Marajó Is.
Nevado Huascarán 22,132
CORD. ORIENTAL
CORDILLERA OCCIDENTAL
Madeira
Paresis Tableland
Guaporé
Tapajós
Xingu
Araguaia
Tocantins
Paraíba
C. de Sao Roque
Fernando de Noronha
BORBOREMA PLATEAU
Paulo Afonso Falls
SOUTH
L. Titicaca
Nevado Sajama 21,463
L. Poopó
Gulf of Arica
Mamoré
Río de la Plata Basin
PLATEAU OF MATO GROSSO
BRAZILIAN HIGHLANDS
Sao Francisco
B. de Todos os Santos
PACIFIC
Tropic of Capricorn
Pilcomayo
Paraguay
Paraná
Pico da Bandeira 9482
Llullaillaco 22,057
Bermejo
Iguazu Falls
Cape Frío
OCEAN
Mt Pissis 22,286
Salado
Gran Chaco
Paraná
Uruguay
CUCHILLA GRANDE
Patos Lagoon
SOUTH
Mt. Aconcagua 22,841
Tupungato 21,490
Pampas
Mirim Lagoon
Río de la Plata
ATLANTIC
Juan Fernández
Colorado
Cape San Antonio
Lanín 12,388
Negro
Bahía Blanca
L. Nahuel Huapi
Valdés Pen.
Chiloé Is.
OCEAN
Gulf of San Jorge
Taitao Pen.
L. Buenos Aires
Argentine Sea
Mt. Fitz Roy 11,020
Bahía Grande
Falkland Is.
L. Argentino
Tierra del Fuego
I. de los Estados
South Georgia
Cape Horn
Drake Passage

A N D E S

KEY

Altitude (in feet)

	13,000 or over
	6500
	1600
	650
	0
	-650 (depression)

Depth (in feet)

	0
	-650
	-6500
	-16,500 or over

0   Scale   1000 miles

80°   60°   40°   20°   0°   20°

SOUTH AMERICA
POLITICAL MAP

NORTH
PACIFIC
OCEAN

NORTH
ATLANTIC
OCEAN

Lesser Antilles

Margarita Is.
(Ven.)

Trinidad

Barranquilla
Maracaibo
Caracas
Valencia

VENEZUELA

Medellín

Georgetown
GUYANA
Paramaribo
SURINAME
Cayenne
FRENCH
GUIANA

Cali
Bogotá

COLOMBIA

0°   Galápagos Is.
(Ecuador)

Equator

0°

Quito
ECUADOR

Guayaquil

Belém
São Luís

Fernando
de Noronha
(Brazil)

Manaus

Fortaleza

Chiclayo

Natal

Recife

B R A Z I L

Maceió

PERU

Salvador

Lima

BOLIVIA

Brasília

La Paz
Arequipa
Cochabamba

SOUTH

Sucre

Belo Horizonte

20°

PARAGUAY

Rio de Janeiro

PACIFIC

Antofagasta

Salta

Asunción
Ciudad del Este

São Paulo

Tropic of Capricorn

CHILE

San Miguel
de Tucumán

Florianópolis

Santa Fe
Córdoba

Porto Alegre

SOUTH

OCEAN

Valparaíso

Salto
URUGUAY

Santiago de Chile

Buenos Aires
La Plata

Montevideo

Juan
Fernández
(Chile)

ARGENTINA

ATLANTIC

Bahía Blanca

Valdivia

Viedma

Chiloé Is.

Rawson

OCEAN   40°
20°

40°

Comodoro Rivadavia

100°

Falkland Is.
(UK)

Río Gallegos

South
Georgia
(UK)

0   Scale   1000 miles

80°   60°   40°   20°

20°

80°   60°   40°

FLORA AND FAUNA

South America boasts a wide range of landscapes and environments. In the tropical forests, there is a rich diversity of animal and plant life, while very different organisms survive in the cold south, or high in the Andes Mountains.

Water lilies in the Wetlands of Pantanal, Brazil.

AMAZON BASIN

Abundance of Life

The largest rain forest in the world lies around the giant Amazon River. More species of animal and plant live here than anywhere else on the planet. The Amazon is the second-longest river in the world, but the largest in terms of volume of water. It contains 20 percent of all the river water in the world.

DESERT SCRUB ANDES – PATAGONIA

Tough Species

This dry environment extends from Colombia in the north to Argentina in the south. It follows the Andes Mountains and includes regions of high **plateau** and the coastal deserts of Chile and Peru. Vegetation is mostly grassland. The animals living here have adapted to survive in tough conditions.

DIVERSITY THE ANDES MOUNTAINS

High Living

The mountain landscape includes dry areas with sparse vegetation and forested areas, such as the Yungas in Bolivia. Many different species of tree grow in the mountain forests. The condor, the Andean flamingo, and the guanaco (a large mammal similar to a camel) can be found in the Andes.

Buzzard Eagle
This bird of prey has special feathers that stop it from freezing to death when it flies over the Andes.

Guianan Cock-of-the-rock
This beautiful bird lives in high rocky areas. It feeds mainly on fruit.

FINE WOOL
Alpacas grow high-quality wool, which is excellent for knitting warm clothing.

Alpaca
The alpaca is very common on the high plains of Ecuador, Bolivia, Chile, and Peru.

Carnivore
The leopard seal is one of the largest predators in the Southern Ocean.

Snake
The red-tailed boa lives in northern South America.

Piranhas
There are several species of piranha in the Amazon River. These **carnivorous** fish can sometimes come together into large schools to attack their prey. However, they rarely attack humans.

Iguanas and Crabs
The Barrington Land iguana (left) and the red rock crab (below) both live on the Galapagos Islands. This remote group of islands in the Pacific Ocean has many unique species. Studying the animals and plants here helped Charles Darwin to formulate his theory of evolution by natural selection.

Patagonian Woods
Larch, myrtle, and monkey puzzle (above, from left to right) are three of the trees found in Patagonia. Below are the most common plant species that grow there:

1. Verbena
2. Antarctic beech
3. Larch
4. Myrtle
5. Lenga beech
6. Monkey puzzle
7. Hazel

CRISIS IN THE AMAZON

One-fifth of the Amazon Rain Forest has been cut down by humans since 1970. However, there are encouraging signs that the rate of destruction is slowing down, as the governments of Brazil and other countries take action. Further destruction of the Amazon could damage the whole world's climate.

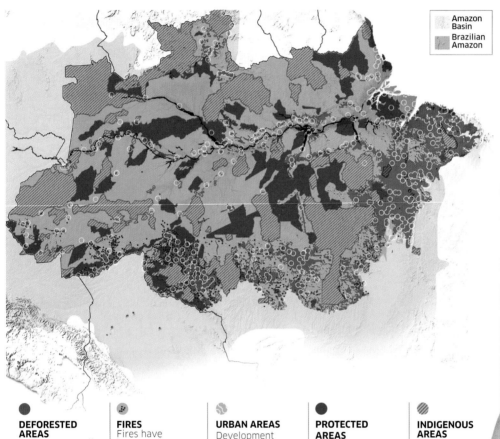

Amazon Basin
Brazilian Amazon

DEFORESTED AREAS
In these areas all the trees have been cut down.

FIRES
Fires have been used to clear land for agriculture.

URBAN AREAS
Development of urban areas is unplanned and growing.

PROTECTED AREAS
National parks that cannot be cut down.

INDIGENOUS AREAS
These areas have some protection.

WHAT IS AT STAKE?
ISSUES THAT AFFECT US ALL

Oxygen
Plants in the Amazon produce about 20 percent of oxygen on Earth. They act like the "lungs of the planet."

Greenhouse Effect
Trees absorb carbon dioxide from the air, slowing down global warming. Without the rain forest, the planet will get hotter more quickly.

Biodiversity
An estimated 10 percent of all the known species of plant and animal live in the Amazon Basin.

Culture
It is thought that about 200,000 indigenous people live in the area. Their diverse cultures could be lost.

AMAZON BASIN
MANY COUNTRIES

A Huge Area

The Amazon Basin extends across an area of about 2.7 million square miles crossing several countries. Half of the rain forest lies in Brazil. The rest is spread across Peru, Bolivia, Colombia, Venezuela, Guyana, and Suriname.

Aerial view
The Amazon River empties approximately 261,590 cubic yards of water into the ocean every second.

Rate of Loss

By 1991, the Amazon had lost 160,232 square miles of forest. By 2000, that number had risen to 226,642 square miles. The cleared land is used to graze livestock and to grow crops. The rate of loss has been slowing in recent years.

People in Danger

Many small groups of people call the Amazon home, such as the Yanomami (pictured left). These groups are in danger of losing their way of life, and with it, a huge amount of knowledge about the forest and its plants will be lost.

Rubber

Rubber trees are grown along the banks of the Tapajós River in Brazil. The rubber is collected from cuts made in the bark.

POPULATION

Many people across South America are moving from the countryside to the cities. This has caused rapid and disorganized growth as makeshift homes are built on the outskirts of large cities. These poor urban areas are known as favelas, or shantytowns.

Rio de Janeiro
A view of this Brazilian city, home to more than 6 million people.

Carnival

In Brazil, the biggest and most important festival is called Carnival. People take to the streets in ornate costumes to have a huge party.

BRAZIL
PORTO ALEGRE

Skyscrapers and Highways

Porto Alegre is the capital city of the state of Rio Grande do Sul. It has a population of nearly 1.5 million and is a center for industry and business.

Salvador da Bahia

The first capital city of Portugal's New World Empire, Salvador was founded in 1549. It is one of the oldest cities in Brazil. The historic city center has been made a UNESCO World Heritage Site. It has a population of about 3 million people.

VENEZUELA
CARACAS

Booming City

With a population of more than 3.5 million inhabitants, Caracas is the ninth-largest urban area in Latin America. It is a commercial center that sees a lot of investment from Venezuelan companies and also from abroad.

COLOMBIA
BOGOTA

Cultural Center

Colombia's main museums and most important universities are found in its capital city, Bogota. It has a population of more than 6.5 million people. Below is an image of the historic Church of St. Francis in the city.

La Boca
A suburb of the city of Buenos Aires, the capital of Argentina.

ARGENTINA
CORDOBA

Second City

The second-largest city in Argentina after Buenos Aires, Cordoba has a population of 1.3 million people. It is known as "the learned one" because the country's best university is found there. Below is the city's cathedral.

Mate
A popular drink in Argentina.

CHILE
SANTIAGO DE CHILE

High Life Expectancy

With a population of more than 5 million people, Chile's capital city, Santiago, is the largest city in the country. The city contains a rich mix of fine old and striking new architecture. Chile is the country with the longest life expectancy in South America, at around 79 years.

ECONOMIC RESOURCES

South America produces a lot of food for export to other parts of the world. It also has many natural resources and some of the largest oil reserves on the planet. Brazil has the largest economy in South America, followed by Argentina, Colombia, Venezuela, Peru, and Chile.

ARGENTINA
TOURISM

Favorite Destination

The Perito Moreno Glacier is a popular tourist attraction. The drive to the glacier from El Calafate takes in a series of lakes, streams, woods, and snow-capped mountains.

Wonder
The huge glacier is a spectacular natural wonder.

VENEZUELA
OIL

Important Reserve

Oil is the main source of income in Venezuela. Today, a state-owned company manages the country's reserves, which are among the largest in the world. As of January 2011, it had 297 billion barrels left (1 barrel = 42 gallons). In 1960, Venezuela was one of the founding members of OPEC, an association of oil producers around the world. It also has reserves of natural gas, methane, iron, gold, and diamonds. Venezuelan industry concentrates on oil refinery and petrochemicals, which are chemicals made using oil. Its exports are mainly products made from oil or steel. It also has textile, timber, and pharmaceutical industries.

URUGUAY
AGRICULTURE AND TOURISM

Sunflowers

The second-smallest country in South America, Uruguay is known for its fine beaches, such as Punta del Este. Its economy is based around cattle farming and other agriculture. Among the crops grown are soy, wheat, barley, oats, rice, corn, and sunflowers (below).

Maracaibo
A center for oil production.

Taking Full Advantage

Mining is the most important industry in Chile, in particular copper mining, which is very profitable. Pictured left is the Chuquicamata mine in the Atacama Desert. Wine-making is another important industry, and Chile exports wine around the world. A typical Chilean vineyard is shown below.

Chuquicamata This is an open-pit mine.

BRAZIL AND COLOMBIA
COFFEE AND MUCH MORE

Powerful Economies

Brazil has traditionally been a large producer of coffee. However, a growing financial sector means that the service sector is now the largest part of the economy, followed by industry. Colombia is still a large producer and exporter of coffee.

Exploitation The Amazon has lost much of its forests, cut down to make way for human activity.

BOLIVIA
ABUNDANT NATURAL GAS

Source of Energy

Bolivia has the second-largest reserves of natural gas in South America. It exports the gas to its neighbors, in particular Brazil and Argentina. It also has smaller oil reserves and many different minerals are mined. The picture below shows some typical gas tankers.

THE NAZCA LINES

The Nazca Lines are drawings on the land in south Peru, some of them more than 984 feet long. They are line drawings of animals, plants, and geometric shapes, which can be seen only from a great height. The lines were drawn on the plain and on the hillsides by the Nazca people, who lived there between 200 BC and AD 500.

PERU
NAZCA

Location

The lines are found in the provinces of Palpa and Nazca on the Pampas de Jumana.

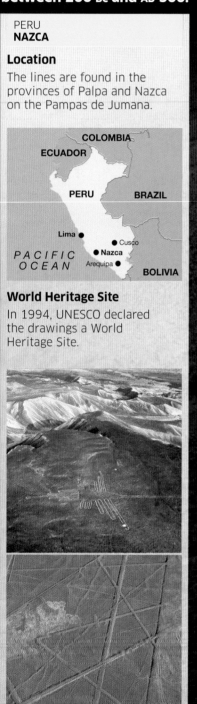

COLOMBIA
ECUADOR
PERU   BRAZIL
Lima
Cusco
PACIFIC   Nazca
OCEAN   Arequipa
BOLIVIA

World Heritage Site

In 1994, UNESCO declared the drawings a World Heritage Site.

Entry and exit

The Spider has an entrance and an exit, which allow you to follow the lines without ever crossing from one line to another.

Strange features

The shape and features of the Spider show that it is based on a species from the Amazon Rain forest.

The Spider
One of the best-known figures, the Spider, is made from one continuous line.

Anthony F. Aveni

A scientist from the USA, Aveni linked the lines to water supplies. He believed that they were used in rituals to secure water for crops.

LEGACY OF THE NAZCA

Cultural Works

The Nazca were fine craftspeople. They made good cloths and their pottery was the best in pre-Columbian South America.

Head Trophy
This trophy was found in a tomb.

Two-Headed Snake
A sacred symbol commonly found in the Andes.

Siku
The Siku is a traditional Andean musical instrument.

Cemetery

Nearby, there is a cemetery dating from pre-Columbian times. This mummy was found there.

Map of the Stars

Some researchers, such as Maria Reiche, have suggested that the Spider is a representation of the star formation Orion.

The ground
The surface is covered with a layer of dark reddish stones.

The Spider. Viewed from the air.

BUENOS AIRES

A fascinating city, Buenos Aires is the most densely populated city in Argentina. In the center of the city, there are many historical buildings next to the Plate River. At Puerto Madero nearby, there are stunningly modern developments.

SYMBOLS OF THE CITY

The Teatro Colón

This magnificent concert hall has some of the best **acoustics** in the world. This means that the audience can hear the music clearly.

Avenida 9 de Julio

At 459 feet wide, this is one of the widest streets in the world. The Obelisk, a famous monument, stands at the junction with Corrientes Avenue.

Town Hall

This building has stood for nearly all of the country's 200 years of independence.

The Frigate Sarmiento

This ship from the Argentinian navy saw service between 1898 and 1961. Today, it is a museum.

Country	Argentina
Area	78 sq mi
Population	2,891,082
Density	37,073 people/sq mi

Night Scene
Puerto Madero has striking new developments, restaurants, and homes.

Puerto Madero
The old port area has seen massive development, with a new residential district and a business center.

NAME
Puerto Madero is named after Eduardo Madero, who drew up the original plans for the port in 1882.

CULTURE IN BUENOS AIRES

Museums

The city has a wide range of museums, including the Proa (top), the Malba (bottom), the Museum of the Fine Arts, and the Museum of Modern Art.

Lezama Park

This park was once a farm owned by the Lezama family. It contains a wide range of different trees, winding paths, a large pergola, waterfalls, monuments, stairways, and an amphitheater.

Underground

The city's underground railroad system has six lines. The first station opened in 1913. It was the first underground to be built in South America and is one of the busiest in the world.

CHRIST THE REDEEMER

The majestic statue of Christ the Redeemer stands with arms outstretched over the center of Rio de Janeiro in Brazil. It is built on the rocky summit of Mount Corcovado, 2326 feet above sea level. It is surrounded by the Tijuca Forest, the largest area of urban woodland in the world.

CHRIST THE REDEEMER
FACT FILE

Height:
125 feet

Outer covering:
Greenish-gray soapstone

Weight:
635 tons

Interior:
The structure is made of hollow reinforced concrete

CULTURAL AND RELIGIOUS WORK

Historical Facts

The statue took five years to build and was opened on October 12, 1931. It was a technical challenge because the area is very windy, and it was very difficult to build the outstretched arms and the bent head. The project was run by the engineer Heitor da Silva Costa. The artist Carlos Oswald came up with the final design, while the sculptor Paul Landowski (below) made the head and the hands.

Coating
Soapstone from Minas Gerais was chosen because bad weather and changes in temperature do not damage it.

Church
At the foot of the statue is a small church.

Height
From the base
to the head it is
125 feet, including
the 26-foot plinth.

Head
The head is bent
downward slightly.

2003
The year that
escalators were
installed to carry
people to the base
of the statue.

Symbol
The imposing statue
is one of the largest
religious images in
the world and has
become a symbol
of Brazil.

Interior
Contains beams
and staircases.

Arms
The arms
span 92 feet.

Mountain Train
The Corcovado Railway
was opened in 1884.
Trains climb through
the lush Tijuca Forest at
a steady 7.4 mi/h. The
trains carried the pieces
of the statue up to the
top of the mountain.

THE AMERICAS
GEOGRAPHICAL WONDERS

Mountains, high plateaus, vast plains, deserts, jungles, volcanoes, and glaciers: North, Central, and South America offer a series of spectacular and varied landscapes. There are also large areas of land that are still untouched by humans, many of them now protected as World Heritage Sites.

ALBERTA
CANADA

Banff National Park

Bow Lake in Banff National Park, Alberta, freezes over every winter. Covering an area of 2564 square miles, the park is home to glaciers, woods, and mountains. UNESCO has declared the park a World Heritage Site.

Glacier landscape
Tire tracks run over the surface of a frozen lake near the Canadian Rockies.

CANADA TO NEW MEXICO
UNITED STATES

The Rocky Mountains

This mountain range extends for more than 3000 miles from northern Canada to New Mexico in the south. A young mountain range, it was formed from a series of separate mountain chains that joined together. Between the peaks, the valleys are home to spectacular forests and lakes.

CALIFORNIA
UNITED STATES

San Andreas Fault

The North American and Pacific tectonic plates collide at the San Andreas Fault, which runs parallel to the coast of California and through the city of San Francisco. It is a very unstable area, prone to devastating earthquakes.

CANADA
NORTH AMERICA

Canadian Shield

The Canadian Shield is an ancient chain of eroded mountains that runs alongside Hudson Bay. It forms the shape of a huge horseshoe and has an average height of 984 feet.

CENTRAL AMERICA AND THE CARIBBEAN

Irazu Volcano

With a height of 11,260 feet, Irazu is the highest active volcano in Costa Rica. The summit has five craters. One of the craters is filled with a green lake (left).

Sierra Maestra

Surrounded by lush vegetation, the Sierra Maestra is a mountain chain in southeastern Cuba. Pico Turquino is the highest peak in the Sierra Maestra, reaching 6476 feet above sea level.

Punta Cana
An area of beautiful beaches on the east coast of the Dominican Republic.

SOUTH AMERICA
AMAZON BASIN

The Great River

The Amazon is the largest river in the world (by volume of water). About 200 smaller rivers flow into it emptying it into the Atlantic Ocean through a huge delta. From the Andes, it flows 4186 miles across South America.

Atacama Desert

The Atacama is one of the driest places on the planet. It extends through the north of Chile between the Copiapo River and the Loa River. Parts of the desert contain rock formations that look like the surface of the Moon.

ARGENTINA
EL CALAFATE

Perito Moreno Glacier

Measuring 18.6 miles long and 3 miles wide, the Perito Moreno Glacier is found in the province of Santa Cruz. Every now and then, there are spectacular crashes of ice as large chunks fall off the front of the glacier.

PEOPLE AND LANGUAGES

Spanish and English are the most widely-spoken languages in the Americas. French and Portuguese are also spoken, as are a wide range of indigenous languages, such as Quechua, Guarani, and Mapuche.

Spanish

Spanish was introduced by the Conquistadors. Since then, the language of each region has changed, developing its own vocabulary and accent.

ORIGINS
The population of the Americas is descended mainly from Amerindians, Africans, and Europeans.

English
The main language of science, trade, and diplomacy.

Culture

Many smaller cultures across the world are in danger of disappearing. Along with them, their languages are lost.

Saving Languages
Anthropologists

believe that it is vital to save languages because they give us different ways of seeing the world.

ORIGINAL LANGUAGES OF THE AMERICAS

Canada and the United States

There are more than 300 native languages, but many are in the process of dying out.

1. Algonquian-Ritwan
2. Caddo
3. Hokan
4. Iroquois
5. Kiowa-Tano
6. Muskogee
7. Others

Mexico and Central America

Quiche and Yucatec are Mayan languages that are still spoken. Many others have disappeared.

1. Macro-Chibcha
2. Maya
3. Mixe-Zoque
4. Oto-Manguean
5. Totonac
6. Uto-Aztecan
7. Others

South America

More than 1000 languages have died out. Some, such as Quechua, are still spoken.

1. Arawak
2. Carib
3. Macro-Chibcha
4. Macro-Ge
5. Pano-Tacanan
6. Quechumaran
7. Others

MAIN NATIVE LANGUAGES
IMPORTANT FACTS

PERU
QUECHUA

Widely Spoken Language

Peru has a great ethnic diversity. Quechua, the language spoken by the Incas, is the language most spoken. It is also spoken in Bolivia, Ecuador, Colombia, Argentina, and Chile.

MEXICO
NAHUATL

A Range of Languages

In Mexico, about 6 million people speak a range of more than 60 native languages. Nahuatl, the Mayan languages, and Zapotec are the most common.

CHILE
MAPUCHE

Influence

The Mapuche, also known as the Araucanians, live in southern Chile and southwest Argentina. Many of their neighbors adopted their language.

CARIBBEAN
CREOLE

African Roots

In Haiti and Dominique, most people speak Creole, which is a language that mixes French vocabulary with the grammar of West African languages.

EUROPE INTRODUCTION

Europe is home to many different people, languages, and cultures. Its cities are rich in history, architecture, and art. The landscape ranges from the towering Alps and Pyrénées to beautiful beaches on the Mediterranean Sea. Most European countries have some valuable natural resources, and many of their people enjoy a high standard of living.

MOUNTAIN BARRIER
THE PYRÉNÉES SEPARATE THE IBERIAN PENINSULA FROM THE REST OF CONTINENTAL EUROPE.

EUROPE
PHYSICAL MAP

Denmark Strait

Cape Horn

Cape Reykjanaes Iceland Cape Fontur

Arctic

Circle

Cape Dyrhólaey

Jan Ma

Faroe Is.

Shetland Is. Cape
Stadlandet

NC

NORTH ATLANTIC OCEAN

Isles

British

Hebrides

Orkney Is.

Grampians

Greenwich Meridian

Erris Head

Penines

NORTH

SEA

Dunmore Head ▲ Carrauntoohil
3415

Irish
Sea

St George's Channel Cambrian
Mts

London
Basin

Frisian Is.

Thames

Strait of Dover

Rhine

English Channel

Ardennes

Rhenish Mas

Pointe St-Mathieu

Seine

Vosges

Black Forest

Belle Isle

Loire

Paris
Basin

Rhine

L. Constance

40°

Cape Finisterre

Bay of
Biscay

Montes
de León

Cantabrian Mts

Dordogne

Loire

L. Geneva

▲ Mt. Blanc
15,781

Minho

Garonne

PYRENEES

Massif
Central

Rhône

Douro

Ebro

Gulf of
Genoa

Sistema Central

Aneto
11,168

Côte d'Azur

Tagus

Iberian

Costa Brava

Corsica

Cape Roca

Guadiana

Peninsula

B. of Setúbal

Sierra Morena

Gulf of
Valencia

Menorca

Cape St Vincent

Guadalquivir

Mallorca

Sardinia

Ibiza

Balearic Islands

Gulf of Cádiz

Baetic Mountains

▲ Mulhacén
11,421

TYR

Strait of Gibraltar

Cape de Gata

MEDITERRAN

Scale

0 000 miles

0°

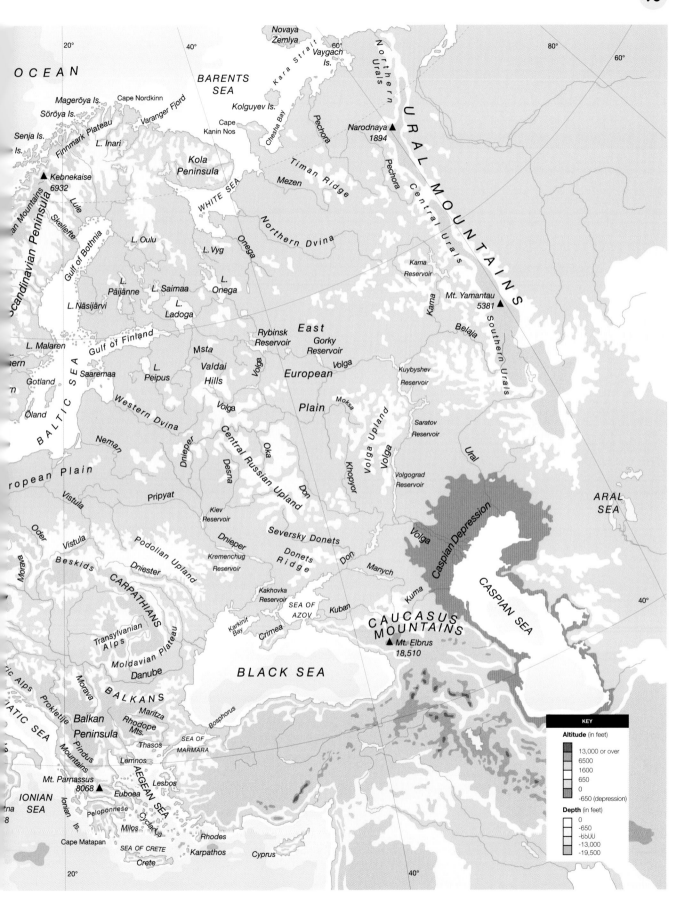

OCEAN

20° 40° 60° 80° 60°

Novaya Zemlya

Vaygach Is.

BARENTS SEA

Kara Strait

Magerøya Is.
Cape Nordkinn
Söröya Is.
Varanger Fjord
Senja Is.
Finnmark Plateau
L. Inari

Kolguyev Is.

Chesha Bay

Cape Kanin Nos

Pechora

Northern Urals

Narodnaya 1894

URAL MOUNTAINS

Central Urals

Kebnekaise 6932

Scandinavian Peninsula

Lule
Skellefte

Kola Peninsula

WHITE SEA

Timan Ridge

Mezen

Pechora

Northern Dvina

Kama Reservoir

Kama

Belaja

Mt. Yamantau 5381

Southern Urals

L. Oulu

Onega

L. Vyg

Gulf of Bothnia

L. Päijänne
L. Näsijärvi

L. Saimaa

L. Onega

L. Ladoga

Gulf of Finland

Rybinsk Reservoir

East

Gorky Reservoir

Kuybyshev Reservoir

L. Malaren

Saaremaa

Msta

Valdai Hills

European

Volga

Plain

Moksa

Saratov Reservoir

Gotland

BALTIC SEA

L. Peipus

Western Dvina

Volga

Volga Upland

Öland

Neman

Dnieper

Desna

Central Russian Upland

Oka

Khopyor

Volga

Ural

ARAL SEA

ropean Plain

Vistula

Pripyat

Kiev Reservoir

Don

Volgograd Reservoir

Caspian Depression

Volga

Oder

Vistula

Podolian Upland

Dniester

Dnieper

Kremenchug Reservoir

Seversky Donets

Donets Ridge

Don

Manych

Kuma

CASPIAN SEA

40°

Morava

Beskids

CARPATHIANS

Kakhovka Reservoir

SEA OF AZOV

Kuban

Karkinit Bay

Crimea

CAUCASUS MOUNTAINS

Mt. Elbrus 18,510

ic Alps

Transylvanian Alps

Moldavian Plateau

Danube

BLACK SEA

Morava

BALKANS

Bosphorus

atic SEA

Prokletije

Balkan Peninsula

Pindus Mountains

Maritza

Rhodope Mts.

Thasos

SEA OF MARMARA

Lemnos

Mt. Parnassus 8068

AEGEAN SEA

Lesbos

IONIAN SEA

Euboea

Ionian Is.

Peloponnese

Cyclades

Milos

Rhodes

Cape Matapan

SEA OF CRETE

Karpathos

Cyprus

Crete

20° 40°

KEY

Altitude (in feet)

13,000 or over
6500
1600
650
0
-650 (depression)

Depth (in feet)

0
-650
-6500
-13,000
-19,500

EUROPE
POLITICAL MAP

60° 40° 20°

ARC

Denmark Strait

Búdardalur
Reykjavik ◉ **ICELAND** • Vopnafjördur
• Höfn

Arctic
Circ

*Faroe Islands
(Denmark)*

Ales

Bergen

British Isles

Stavanger
Kristians

• Aberdeen

*NORTH
ATLANTIC OCEAN*

• Glasgow

IRELAND
Belfast •
**UNITED
KINGDOM**

*NORTH
SEA*

DE

Dublin ◉
• Manchester

Liverpool •

• Oxford

NETHERLANDS

London ◉ The Hague • ◉ **Amsterdam**
Rotterdam •

BELGIUM
GEF

Brussels ◉

LUXEMBOURG
Luxembo

Brest •
• Le Havre

S

◉ **Paris**

40°

Nantes •
• Dijon

FRANCE

• Limoges

Bern ◉ Zurich

La Coruña •

SWITZERLA

• Bordeaux
Lyon •

Oporto •
Bilbao •

• Turin

• Toulouse

MONACO
Geno

Viseu •
• Salamanca

ANDORRA
Andorra
la Vella

Nice •

SAN M

PORTUGAL

Madrid ◉
Marseille •

Bastia •

Lisbon ◉
Setúbal •

• Badajoz **S P A I N**

Corsica

VA

• Girona

• Córdoba

• Barcelona

Sassari •

• Seville

Palma de
Mallorca •
Ibiza • Menorca
Mallorca

Sardinia

Cádiz •
• Cartagena

Balearic Islands
• Cagliari

• Marbella

M E D I T E R R A N E A N

P

Scale

0 **600 miles**

AFRICA

0°

20°   40°   60°   80°   60°

N

Novaya Zemlya

BARENTS SEA

• Pechora

ASIA

Vardö •
• Murmansk

Narvik •   • Inari

odö •   • Rovaniemi

• Gällivare
• Arkhangelsk

• Lulea
• Syktyvkar

• Storuman   Oulu   **FINLAND**   • Belomorsk

Östersund •   • Vaasa   • Kuopio
• Perm

• Borlänge   • Tampere   • Petrozavodsk
R U S S I A

Kotka •   *(European area)*

arlstad   Turku •   ◉ **Helsinki**

ockholm ◉   • St Petersburg
• Kazan

ourg   ◉ **Tallinn**
• Samara

mar •   **ESTONIA**   • Tver

BALTIC SEA   Tartu •   • Moscow ◉
• Saratov

ö •   **LATVIA**   ◉ Riga

ARAL SEA

Siauliai •   • Daugavpils

LITHUANIA   • Vitebsk   • Smolensk

Gdynia •   **RUSSIA**   ◉ **Vilnius**   • Borysaw
• Volgograd

• Kaliningrad   • Grodno   ◉ **Minsk**   • Kursk
• Astrakhan

Szczecin •   **BELARUS**
CASPIAN SEA

POLAND   • Pinsk
40°

Warsaw ◉   • Kiev ◉
• Kharkiv

• Walbrzych   Lublin •   Rivne •   • Zhytomyr
• Rostov

• Kraków   **UKRAINE**   • Donetsk

ECH
• Stavropol

UBLIC   **SLOVAKIA**   **MOLDOVA**
• Makhachkala

a •   ◉ **Bratislava**   • Mukachevo   ◉ **Chisinau**   • Sochi

◉ **Budapest**   • Odessa
• Sebastopol

HUNGARY   **ROMANIA**

NIA   • Timisoara
BLACK SEA

jana   ◉ Zagreb

BOSNIA AND   ◉ **Belgrade**   ◉ **Bucharest**

HERZEGOVINA   Giurgiu •   • Varna

Sarajevo   **SERBIA**   **BULGARIA**

MONTENEGRO   **KOSOVO**   ◉ Sofia

Podgorica •   ◉ **Pristina**   • Plovdiv

◉ **Skopje**   ◉ **Istanbul**

Tirana •   **MACEDONIA**

ALBANIA   • Thessaloniki   **TURKEY**
A S I A

aranto •   *(European area)*

GREECE

Reggio   Patras •   ◉ **Athens**
• Piraeus

cuse   Kalamata •

a

TA

Heraklion •
Crete

20°   40°

GEOGRAPHICAL WONDERS

Europe is the second-smallest continent in the world after Oceania. It is mostly very flat, with an average height of just 984 feet. However, the mountain ranges of Europe, such as the Pyrenees, the Alps, and the Caucasus, reach as high as 18,510 feet.

ATLANTIC HEIGHTS
SCANDINAVIA AND ICELAND

High Peaks

The highest peaks in northern Europe are found in Scandinavia. Mount Galdhøpiggen, in Norway, is the highest in the region at 8100 feet.

Alpine Ranges
Typical Alpine landscapes have lakes surrounded by snow-capped peaks.

WESTERN EUROPE
ITALY–FRANCE

Mont Blanc

The most famous peak in Europe is Mont Blanc. Officially, it is 15,781 feet high. However, the layer of snow at the summit can add between 33-49 feet, depending on the time of year. The peak lies on the border between France and Italy.

SPAIN
LA MANCHA

Spain's Central Plains

La Mancha is the largest plain on the Iberian Peninsula. The plain is split in two by the mountains of Toledo. The highest summits are Villuercas, at 5253 feet, and Rocigalgo, at 4747 feet. The area is famed for its traditional windmills.

RUSSIA
GLACIAL LAKES

The Valdai Plateau

The Valdai plateau is located halfway between the Russian cities of St. Petersburg and Moscow. The great plateau is drained by the Volga and Dnieper rivers, among others. Throughout the area, there are many beautiful glacial lakes.

CAUCASUS – RUSSIA
MOUNT ELBRUS

Highest Peak

Mount Elbrus is the highest peak in
Europe at 18,510 feet high. The mountain
is located on the northern edge of the
Caucasus Mountains, near the Russian–
Georgian border. Mount Elbrus is a volcano
that has been dormant for more than
2000 years. Its summit is covered by
a permanent layer of ice and more
than 20 glaciers. The mountain is very
popular among skiers and snowboarders.

Mount Elbrus
Located on the border
between Europe and Asia.

RUSSIA
RIVER SYSTEMS

Floodplains

**The gently flowing rivers in
western Russia deposit mud and
rock as they pass by, to create
areas called alluvial floodplains.
The soil in the floodplains is rich
in nutrients and is used to grow all
kinds of crops, including cereals,
potatoes, and beets.**

THE ALPS
IN PROFILE

Mountain chains, such as
the Alps, are formed by
folds and breaks in the
Earth's crust. **Erosion** wears
away the mountains, and
rivers carve valleys that
separate one mountain from
another. High plateaux, such
as the Massif Central in
France, are often found
next to the rocky peaks.

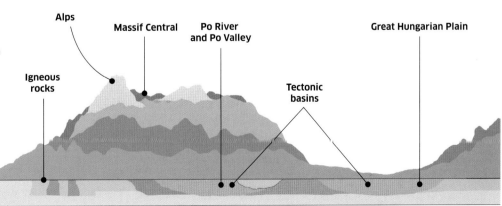

Alps

Massif Central

Po River
and Po Valley

Great Hungarian Plain

Igneous
rocks

Tectonic
basins

Atlantic Ocean

THE ALPS

The Alps is the main mountain range of central Europe. These mountains stretch from Austria and Slovenia in the east, through Italy, Switzerland, Liechtenstein, and Germany to France in the west. With their snow-capped peaks, the Alps have been shaped by thousands of years of glacial erosion.

Snow-capped
The mighty Alpine peaks.

Vulture

The bearded vulture, which is in danger of extinction, has been reintroduced to the Alps.

GLACIERS
Each year, 3 percent of Alpine glacier ice is lost as a result of global warming.

Mountain Goat

This agile animal moves easily around the rocky terrain.

France
Mont Blanc is the highest mountain in the Alps. A 7-mile tunnel runs through the mountain.

Italy
This satellite view shows the Alps in Italy. The mountains cover an area of 115,830 square miles.

SIGHTS
DATA FILE

Facts about the Alps
The Alps is the longest mountain range in Europe. About 16 million people live in the Alpine region.

1 **Length of mountain range:** 746 miles
2 **Ecosystems:** Temperate deciduous forest, alpine pasture
3 **Highest peak:** Mont Blanc (15,781 feet)

Vacations
The slopes offer all kinds of activities, from mountaineering and hiking to snowboarding and skiing.

ITALY
DOLOMITES NATIONAL PARK

Typical Vegetation
The landscape of the Dolomites National Park is dominated by coniferous forests. About 1400 different species of plant grow in the park.

SNOW
SKIING SEASON

Lech–Zürs, Austria
One of Europe's most visited ski resorts, the area's steep slopes and snowy climate mean that its skiing season lasts from November to late April.

ÖTZI
THE ICE MAN

The Mummy and His Weapons
In 1991, the mummified body of a man was found in the ice on the border between Italy and Austria. The body was more than 5000 years old and had been preserved by the ice. The man has been named Ötzi the Ice Man. Next to his body lay his weapons: an ax, a knife, and a bow and arrows.

Studies suggest that Ötzi died during a fight.

THE DANUBE RIVER

Nearly 1800 miles long, the Danube is the second-longest river in Europe. The river supports many different industries, including tourism, fishing, and transportation.

60
out of 300
The number of the Danube's tributaries that are navigable.

MAJOR CITIES ON THE RIVER

Course

The Danube rises in the town of Donaueschingen in Germany's Black Forest. It flows from there to the Black Sea. The river passes through 10 countries: Germany, Austria, Hungary, Slovakia, Croatia, Serbia, Bulgaria, Romania, Moldova, and Ukraine.

POLLUTION
INDUSTRY

Chemicals

The Danube River flows through densely populated and industrialized areas, where there are **nuclear power** plants, factories, and farms. Many chemicals leak into the river, and its waters are badly polluted.

Fishermen

Fishing is an important industry on the Danube. This Romanian fisherman is holding two sturgeon that he caught in the river.

Paris, France
In recent years, the temperatures in European cities have been higher than usual.

20,000
The number of people who died during the European heatwave of 2003.

Heatwave
Between August 3 and 13, 2003, the average temperature in Paris, France, was 104 °F

HEATWAVE
CRISIS IN EUROPE

Consequences

In 2003, there was a **heatwave** throughout Europe. Southern countries, such as Spain, Italy, and Portugal, had the highest temperatures. Alicante in Spain saw temperatures reach 116.6 °F.

France

During the heatwave, temperatures in France reached their highest since 1950. In Paris, the temperature reached 104 °F during the day. The warmest night was on August 11–12, when the temperature only dropped to 78 °F.

Mediterranean

The climate of Portovenere, Italy (left), is extreme. The summers are often incredibly hot and the winters are very cold.

Greece

In winter on the Greek islands, it rains one day in three. However, the sea remains as warm as 59 °F even in the middle of winter.

THE DECIDUOUS FOREST HABITAT

Much of continental Europe is covered in temperate forests. These forests are home to deciduous trees such as oak, beech, and lime. Many animals, small and large, live in the forests, including squirrels, rabbits, wild boar, deer, foxes, eagle owls, and other birds of prey.

BUTTERFLIES
Caterpillars eat the tender leaves of oak and maple trees and many other plants. They then spin their cocoons on the trees before hatching as beautiful butterflies.

Fallow deer
These well-camouflaged deer feed on grasses and acorns found on the forest floor. They live in herds of more than 100.

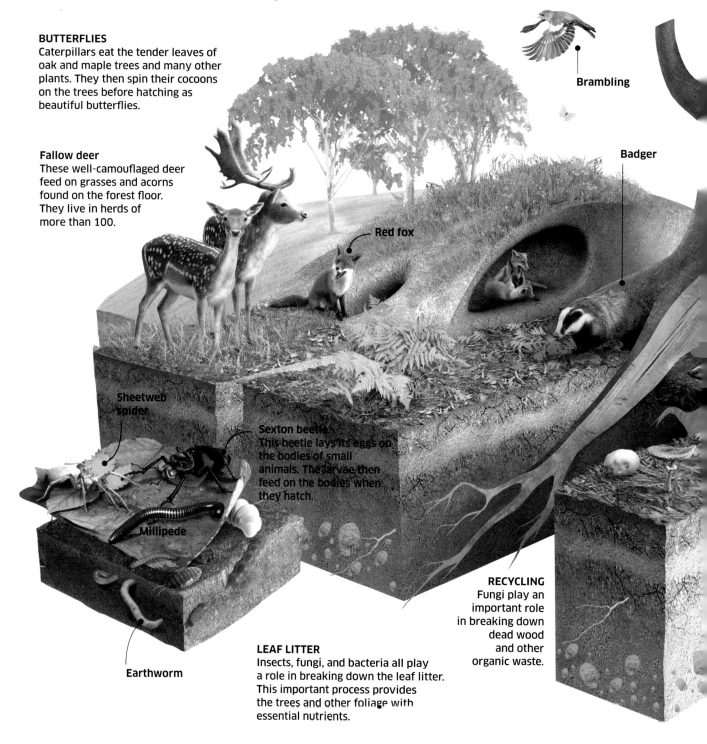

European green woodpecker

Brambling

Badger

Red fox

Sheetweb spider

Sexton beetle
This beetle lays its eggs on the bodies of small animals. The larvae then feed on the bodies when they hatch.

Millipede

Earthworm

LEAF LITTER
Insects, fungi, and bacteria all play a role in breaking down the leaf litter. This important process provides the trees and other foliage with essential nutrients.

RECYCLING
Fungi play an important role in breaking down dead wood and other organic waste.

Gray
squirrel

Common
pipistrelle

Eagle owl
This solitary animal rests during the day
and hunts at night. The eagle owl has
been known to hunt other birds,
including other owls. Its deep cry can
be heard up to 2 miles away.

Wild boar
The wild boar can reach a maximum
weight of 220 pounds. It has
an excellent sense of smell that
it uses to detect food and the
presence of predators.

Pine
marten

Common
hedgehog

Common
pheasant

Edible
dormouse

Rabbit

**BUILDING
TUNNELS**
Rabbits dig complex tunnel
systems, called warrens, in the
forest floor. Each warren has
many entrances and exits.

LIFE
IN THE WOOD

Hibernation

Many mammals, such as bats
(below), sleep during the coldest
weeks of winter. This is called
hibernation. During hibernation,
their body temperature and
breathing are lower than normal.
They use the fat reserves stored
in their bodies during the warmer
months, to survive the winter.

FALL
DECIDUOUS TREES

Falling Leaves

During the fall months, the
deciduous trees of Europe's forests
lose their leaves. Fall starts
in September. New leaves begin
to grow in the spring, which
starts in March.

Turning Brown

Plants need sunlight to produce
the chlorophyll that keeps their
leaves green. With less light in
the fall, the trees stop producing
chlorophyll and the leaves
turn red, brown, and yellow.

POPULATION

In the 1900s, about 25 percent of the world's population lived in Europe. Today, the populations of other continents have grown to overtake Europe, but it is still a densely populated continent. It is mostly very developed, with modern cities and a high standard of living.

City of London
The City is London's financial district. It is lively and full of activity during the day, but much quieter at night.

LONDON, UNITED KINGDOM
A POPULOUS CITY

Business Center
London, the capital of the United Kingdom (UK), is home to about 7.83 million people. Built along the banks of the Thames River, it is a **cosmopolitan** city and world financial center.

Tower Bridge
This striking bridge opened in 1894. The bridge allows vehicles and pedestrians to cross from one side of the Thames River to the other. It also has an electrohydraulic system that enables it to open, to let ships and large vessels travel down the Thames.

Traditions
The UK has managed to balance modern living with the traditions of the past. As a result, the country has a rich and varied cultural heritage.

BELGIUM
BRUSSELS

Home of the European Union

Brussels is one of the most densely populated cities in Europe. The city is the capital of Belgium and also the administrative headquarters of the European Union (EU). Most of the city's inhabitants speak French, while some speak Flemish. The Royal Palace (below) was built in 1779 and is the official residence of the king of Belgium.

BULGARIA
JOINING THE EUROPEAN UNION

Between East and West

For many centuries, Bulgaria was ruled by the **Ottoman Empire**. After World War II, it was close to the Soviet Union. In January 2007, Bulgaria became a member of the **European Union**. The country's main ethnic groups are Bulgarians, Turks, and Roma. The photo below shows Nesebar, an old resort town on the Black Sea, and a peasant in traditional Bulgarian clothes.

ITALY
NAPLES

Picturesque but Troubled

Naples, with about 1 million inhabitants, is the third-largest city in Italy. The city has beautiful historic buildings, but it is plagued by a high rate of unemployment and has a high crime rate.

Naples
A street in the historic center of the city.

Street Sales
A street seller offers rabbits for sale in Naples.

RUSSIAN FEDERATION
MOSCOW

Biggest City

Moscow has over 11.5 million inhabitants, making it the largest city in Europe. Built along the banks of the Moskva River, it is the capital of the Russian Federation. The city contains many fine historical buildings, including the Kremlin (below), a huge fortified palace at the center of the city, which now serves as the official residency of the Russian president.

ECONOMY

Europe's economy is one of the strongest in the world. However, not all the countries in Europe share the same level of development—countries in the west tend to be more developed than those in the east. Trade, transportation, finance, tourism, and heavy industry drive the European economy.

Engadine Valley, Switzerland
The Engadine Valley sits at 5906 feet above sea level. It is surrounded by striking mountains, where skiing is a very popular pastime.

ALPS
TOURISM

Snow Sports

Each year, snow sports attract millions of tourists to the Alps. These visitors provide the Alpine countries with a great economic boost.

Skiing
Skiers flock to the Alps.

TRANSPORTATION NETWORK
RAILROADS

High-Speed Trains

Despite its many natural borders, the European transportation network is highly developed. Due to the growth of trade with the East, the number of passengers and the volume of cargo coming into, and going out of, Europe has greatly increased. To solve the problem of congestion at airports and on highways, the continent has a network of high-speed trains that connects many of Europe's main cities in just a few hours. For example, it is possible to travel from London to Paris in about two hours.

CROPS
PRIMARY SECTOR

Bulgaria's Roses

Roses have been grown in Bulgaria's Rose Valley for centuries. The region is the leading producer of rose oil, which is used in perfumes. Collecting the roses is done by hand, usually by women.

The Eurostar
These trains travel between London, Paris, and Brussels.

Bergheim, Germany
These blast furnaces are used in the production of steel.

FUEL
NATURAL GAS

The Energy Problem

Most European countries have to **import** gas. Around 60 percent of Europe's gas is imported. Most comes from Russia. To avoid having to depend on Russia, many Western European countries are looking to use other energy sources, such as **solar**, wind, and nuclear **power**.

A BLOCK OF NATIONS
UNITY IN EUROPE

The European Union

Most of the countries in Europe belong to the European Union (EU). Citizens of EU countries can travel and work anywhere within the EU. Most of the countries use the euro as currency. As of 2014, the list of countries in the EU are: Austria, Belgium, Bulgaria, Croatia, Cyprus, Czech Republic, Denmark, Estonia, Finland, France, Germany, Greece, Hungary, Ireland, Italy, Latvia, Lithuania, Luxembourg, Malta, Netherlands, Poland, Portugal, Romania, Slovakia, Slovenia, Spain, Sweden, and the United Kingdom.

Car factory
Germany, France, and Italy are the main car manufacturers in Europe.

LOW COUNTRIES
POLDERS

Reclaiming Land

Polders are low-lying pieces of land that are enclosed by barriers called dikes that separate the land from the sea. Water is pumped out of the low-lying land, which dries up and can be used for farming. This technique was first used in the Netherlands in the twelfth century.

LANGUAGES AND PEOPLE

There are three main language groups in Europe: 300 million people speak Slavic languages, such as Russian and Polish, 200 million speak Romance languages, such as French, Italian, and Spanish; and another 200 million people speak Germanic languages, such as English, Swedish, and German.

Protected

Finnish, Hungarian, and Estonian are Uralic languages that are protected as national tongues. Other Uralic languages have been displaced by Russian.

Basque
Basque, spoken in parts of Spain and France, is the only European language that does not belong to the Indo-European group of languages.

Most Spoken

Due to European colonialism between the 16th and 20th centuries, English, Spanish, French, and Portuguese are among the most commonly spoken languages in the world.

Language
Speech is the most versatile form of communication.

Traditional Dress
There were 16 million Muslims living in the EU in 2007, and most are immigrants or the children of immigrants. Many Muslim women cover their heads with a traditional veil.

Immigrants
Immigrants in Europe face many kinds of discrimination. Here, demonstrators in London campaign against the deportation of Nigerian immigrants.

NATIVE LANGUAGES OF EUROPE

Indo-European languages
Almost all European languages are descended from Indo-European languages. These were spoken by Asiatic tribes that invaded Europe 6000 years ago. They gave rise to a number of language families:

1. Albanian
2. Baltic
3. Celtic
4. Slavic
5. Germanic
6. Greek
7. Romance
8. Uralic

Romance Languages
Descended from Latin, which was spread by the Roman Empire:

1. Spanish, or Castilian
2. Catalan
3. French
4. Portuguese
5. Italian
6. Romansh
7. Romanian

Religion
The largest religious groups in Europe are Christian churches:

1. **The Catholic Church**
   Based around the absolute authority of the Pope.

2. **Protestant Churches**
   Anglicans, Calvinists, Lutherans, and others.

3. **Greek and Russian Orthodox Churches**
   Eastern European churches that do not recognize the authority of the Pope.

CASE STUDIES EUROPEAN IDENTITIES

AUSTRIA
AUSTRO-BAVARIAN

German Dialect
The Austro-Bavarian dialect is spoken in Austria and in the southern German state of Bavaria. This dialect is the native tongue of about 12 million people.

SCANDINAVIA
SAMI

Fight for Their Rights
The last aboriginal European culture still survives in remote parts of northern Scandinavia and Russia. The Sami-also known as Lapps-number about 80,000 people.

THE BALKANS
GREECE

Cradle of Civilization
Ancient Greece was one of the great civilizations of history. Today, modern Greeks consider themselves to be Western Europeans, although the country is located in the east of the continent.

ACROSS EUROPE
ROMA

Indian Peoples
Also known as gypsies, the **nomadic** Roma people arrived in Europe from India in the eleventh century. They number about 12 million people.

THE SAMI PEOPLE

The Sami people, or Lapps, are among the oldest inhabitants of Europe. Scattered throughout the **Scandinavian** countries, they total some 80,000 people. The Sami's traditional lifestyle changed first with the arrival of Christianity in the region 1000 years ago, then again with the technological advances of the twentieth century.

FROM AFRICA TO EURASIA

A Common Heritage

The first modern humans left Africa about 80,000 years ago and settled in Oceania and Asia. A second migration took place 35,000 years ago to the Middle East and the Balkans. It is thought that 80 percent of Europeans have **ancestors** who migrated at this time. It is thought that the other 20 percent of Europeans came from the Middle East about 10,000 years ago.

ADAPTATION TO THE CLIMATE

Fair Skin

It is thought that as people moved north from Africa to Europe, they had less exposure to the Sun. As a result, over time, their skin became lighter.

Sami Family
This image from around 1900 shows a Sami family in Lappland.

Culture

The Sami were nomadic people, moving from place to place with herds of reindeer. Most Sami lived in small family groups. Today, they rarely live in this traditional way.

Beliefs

The Sami religion focused on the worship of animal and ancestral spirits. Today, many are Christians and follow Lutheranism.

Tools

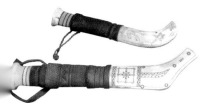

The Sami are skilled craftspeople who carve tools and other implements from bone, wood, antlers, and silver. Their carvings are often decorated with geometric patterns.

Identity

Although the Sami are spread across four countries (Norway, Sweden, Finland, and Russia), they have their own flag (left).

Tents

The tents used by the Sami were similar to North American tepees. They were made from reindeer skins and were easy to take down as the tribe moved from place to place. Today, most of the Sami live in European-style houses.

Economy

Traditionally, the Sami were **hunter-gatherers**. Today, they are reindeer herders, and they are thought to have about half a million reindeer.

Shaman's Drum

The Sami believed that the shaman was a link between them and the spirit world. During ceremonies, the shaman played a drum.

PRAGUE

Located in the heart of Europe, the Czech capital Prague has a rich musical tradition and was home to the famous composer Antonín Dvořák. The city has many tourist attractions, including museums, galleries, churches, synagogues, palaces, and gardens.

Country	Czech Republic
Area	191 sq mi
Population	1,258,106
Density	6587 people/sq mi

SYMBOLS OF THE CITY

Astronomical Clock

Prague's **astronomical clock** dates from the fifteenth century. It is one of the city's best-loved tourist attractions, and hundreds of visitors flock to stand under it each hour, waiting to see it working.

Charles Bridge

This famous bridge unites the old and new cities. It opened in 1503 and is 1693 feet long and 31 feet wide. There are religious statues along it, and those who stand on the bridge get a great view of Prague.

Population

According to 2006 data, 8.77 percent of the population of Prague was foreign-born.

Old Town Square

The Old Town Square is located between Wenceslas Square and Charles Bridge. The north side is dominated by the white facade of the church of Saint Nicholas. The Stone Bell House and the Goltz-Kinsky Palace are on the east side.

PEDESTRIANS
Many streets are pedestrianized. In summer, tables at the sidewalk cafes attract thousands of tourists.

Old Town
Prague's Old Town is free of traffic and surrounded by historic buildings.

TOURIST DESTINATION

Old Town

The first people to arrive in Prague settled in the Old Town. Among the highlights of the Old Town Square is the Astronomical Cock. Across the Vltava River lies the Lesser Town, which is known as Mala Strana in Czech.

Monument to Jan Hus.

Dancing House

This modern building in Prague is nicknamed "Ginger and Fred" after the US dancers Ginger Rogers and Fred Astaire. It is thought to look like a pair of dancers.

Vrtbovska Garden

Dating from 1720, this **terraced garden** has spectacular views of the city. Weddings, concerts, and other events are held in the garden.

THE COLOSSEUM

In the first century AD, the Colosseum was built in Rome by Emperor Vespasian. This **amphitheater** seated up to 50,000 spectators. Today, the ruins of the Colosseum are one of Rome's biggest tourist attractions.

THE COLOSSEUM
FACT FILE

Location:
Rome, Italy

Type:
Amphitheater

Date opened:
AD 80

Capacity:
50,000

Dimensions:

157 ft   617 ft   512 ft   1719 ft

Colossus

It is thought that the Colosseum was named after the colossal statue of Emperor Nero.

MVNIFICENTIA·PII·IX·P·M·

CORINTHIAN COLUMN

IONIC COLUMN

DIFFERENT COLUMNS

Styles

The building had three different types of column, which were used to decorate the outside walls: Doric, Ionic, and Corinthian.

Doric   Ionic   Corinthian

COLOSSEUM **UP CLOSE**

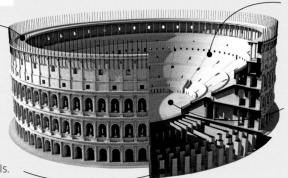

Sliding Roof
A canvas roof protected the public from rain and sun.

Underground
Cells and cages were built underground for the gladiators and wild animals.

Bleachers
Seating was arranged according to social class. The better seats were made from marble, while the top section was made of wood.

Arena
The Colosseum was used for bloody contests including mock sea battles, animal hunts, executions, and dramas based on mythology.

1 MILLION
The number of tons of stone and brick that were used to construct the arches.

Walls
They were raised with blocks of stone, brick, and **limestone**.

Ruins
After a series of earthquakes, much of the building has collapsed.

DORIC COLUMN

Colosseum
The outside view of the amphitheater.

THE ALHAMBRA

This walled city in southern Spain is a beautiful complex of palaces, forts, and gardens. It was home to the court of the Arab (Moorish) kingdom of Granada between the thirteenth and fifteenth centuries. The Alhambra is considered one of the greatest examples of Islamic art in Europe.

THE ALHAMBRA
FACT FILE

Date:
Ninth to fourteenth centuries

Location:
Granada, Spain

Structure:
Originally built for military purposes, the city was both a strong fortress and a palace. The Spanish added other buildings, such as the palace of Charles V.

JOINING THE SQUARES

Patio of the Lions

The garden displays the Muslim idea of Paradise. In each room, there are four waterfalls supported by 12 lions. The columns are joined with lace panels that let in sunlight.

Lion Fountain
Made from marble, this is found in the central courtyard.

10,000
The number of inscriptions that adorn the Alhambra.

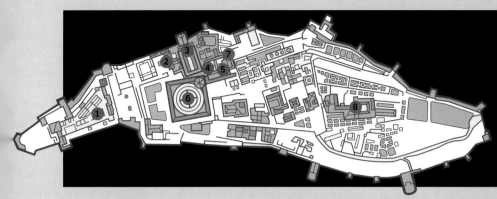

Architectural Plan

1. Alcazaba
2. The Golden Room
3. Comares Palace
4. Palace of the Lions
5. Patio of the Lions
6. Palace of Charles V
7. Hall of the Kings
8. Monastery of St. Francis

Last King

Boabdil was the last king of Moorish Spain. He was overthrown in 1492 by Catholic forces from the north.

Motto
On many of the walls, the **inscriptions** read: "There is no god but Allah."

The Alhambra
View of the building in Granada, southern Spain.

Court of the Myrtles
When the Alhambra was built, water was in short supply, so the large pond here was a symbol of wealth and power. The court is also called the Court of the Pond.

Palace of Charles V
The palace was built in the sixteenth century. It is a **Renaissance**-style double-story building with a large, circular courtyard. Today, it houses the Museum of Fine Arts.

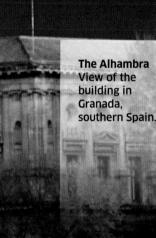

ASIA
INTRODUCTION

Asia makes up one-third of the Earth's continental landmass. The center of the continent is dominated by a large plateau and huge mountain ranges. Great rivers flow across Asia, including the Yangtze in China and the Ganges in India. The Earth's lowest place, the Dead Sea, can be found on the border of Israel and Jordan. The continent also has a great range of peoples. There are many different ethnic groups in Asia, from the Sherpas of the Himalayas, to the Roma. Each of them have their own beliefs, language, and lifestyle.

JORDAN
THE SANDSTONE IN THE REGION NEAR THE ANCIENT CITY OF PETRA IS CARVED INTO UNIQUE ROCK FORMATIONS, SUCH AS THESE CANYONS.

ASIA
PHYSICAL MAP

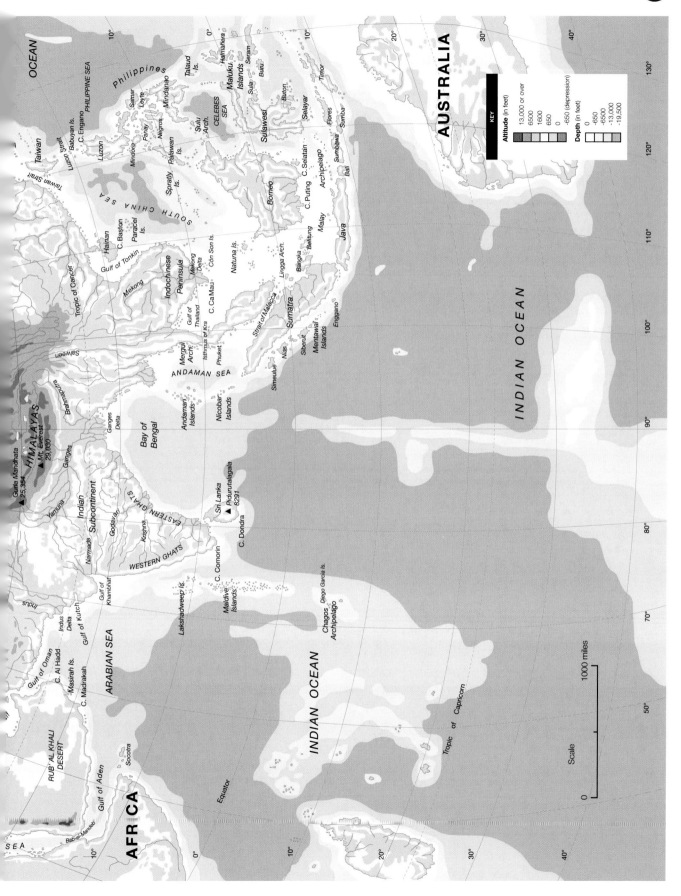

OCEAN

Philippines

PHILIPPINE SEA

Talaud
Is.

Halmahera

Maluku
Islands

Seram

Samar

Leyte

Mindanao

Buru

Sula

CELEBES
SEA

Sulawesi

C. Engano

Babuyan Is.

Luzon Strait

Luzon

Panay

Negros

Sulu
Arch.

C. Selatan

Buton

Selayar

Taiwan Strait

Taiwan

Mindoro

Palawan

Spratly
Is.

Flores

SOUTH CHINA SEA

C. Baston

Parcel
Is.

Borneo

C. Puting

Archipelago

Sumba

Sumbawa

Hainan

Côn Son Is.

Malay

Bali

Java

Gulf of Tonkin

Mekong
Delta

Natuna Is.

Lingga Arch.

Belitung

Enggano

Bangka

Indochinese
Peninsula

Mekong

Gulf of
Thailand

C. Ca Mau

Sumatra

Mekong

Salween

Isthmus of Kra

Strait of Malacca

Phuket

Mergui
Arch.

Siberut

Mentawai
Islands

ANDAMAN SEA

Nias

Simeulue

Brahmaputra

Andaman
Islands

Ganges
Delta

Nicobar
Islands

Gulu Mandhata
▲ 25,354

HIMALAYAS

▲ Mt. Everest
29,030

Bay of
Bengal

Ganges

Ganges

Yamuna

Indian
Subcontinent

Sri Lanka

▲ Pidurutalagala
8291

EASTERN GHATS

Godavari

Krishna

Narmada

C. Dondra

WESTERN GHATS

C. Comorin

Gulf of
Khambhat

Lakshadweep Is.

Indus

Chagos

Diego Garcia Is.

Indus
Delta

Maldive
Islands

Archipelago

Gulf of Kutch

Gulf of Oman

C. Al Hadd

ARABIAN SEA

Masirah Is.

C. Madrakah

RUB' AL KHALI
DESERT

Socotra

AFRICA

Gulf of Aden

Tropic of Cancer

INDIAN OCEAN

INDIAN OCEAN

Tropic of Capricorn

Equator

AUSTRALIA

KEY

Altitude (in feet)

13,000 or over
6500
1600
650
0

Depth (in feet)

0
-650
-6500
-13,000
-19,500

-650 (depression)

Scale

1000 miles

0

Bab-el-Mandeb

SEA

10°

0°

10°

20°

30°

40°

0°

10°

20°

30°

40°

50°

70°

80°

90°

100°

110°

120°

130°

ASIA
POLITICAL MAP

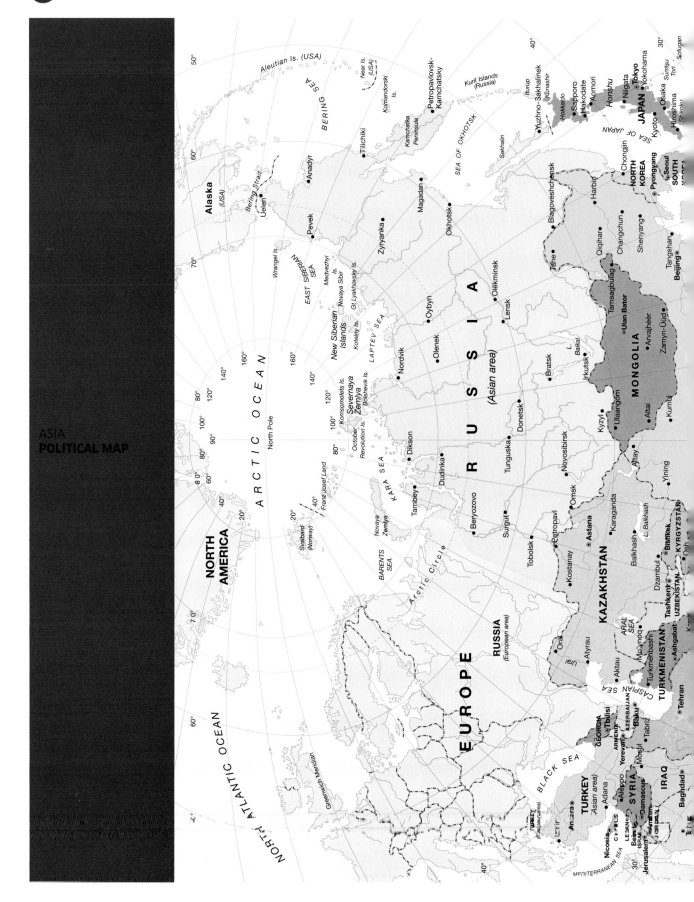

ARCTIC OCEAN

North Pole

50°
60°
70°
80°
120°
140°
160°
100°
90°
80°
60°
40°
20°
70°
60°

Aleutian Is. (USA)

BERING SEA

Near Is. (USA)
Komandorski Is.

Petropavlovsk-Kamchatsky

Kuril Islands (Russia)

Kamchatka Peninsula

SEA OF OKHOTSK

Sakhalin

Iturup
Kunashir
Yuzhno-Sakhalinsk

Hokkaido
Sapporo
Hakodate
Aomori
Honshu
JAPAN
Tokyo
Yokohama
Niigata
Osaka
Kyoto
Hiroshima
Sumisu
Tori
Sofugan
Shikoku
SEA OF JAPAN

Chongjin
NORTH KOREA
Pyongyang
SOUTH
Seoul

Harbin
Blagoveshchensk
Tahe
Qiqihar
Changchun
Shenyang
Tangshan
Beijing

Tamsagbulag
Ulan Bator
Arvaiheer
Zamyn-Üüd
MONGOLIA
Altai
Kumul
Ulaangom
Altay

Tilichiki

Magadan

Okhotsk

Zynyanka

Pevek

Anadyr

Bering Strait

Uelen

Alaska (USA)

Wrangel Is.

EAST SIBERIAN SEA

Medvezhyi Is.
Novaya Sibir
Gt Lyakhovsky Is.
New Siberian Islands
Kotelny Is.

LAPTEV SEA

Olyokminsk
Lensk
Bratsk
Irkutsk
L. Baikal

Oybyn

Olenek

Nordvik

Dikson

Dudinka

Tambey

Beryozovo

Surgut

Komsomolets Is.
Severnaya Zemlya
Bolshevik Is.
October Revolution Is.

KARA SEA

Franz Josef Land

Novaya Zemlya

Svalbard (Norway)

BARENTS SEA

Arctic Circle

R U S S I A
(Asian area)

Donetsk
Tunguska
Novosibirsk
Omsk

Tobolsk
Kostanay

Petropavl
Astana
Karaganda

KAZAKHSTAN
Balkhash
L. Balkhash

Dzambul
Tashkent
UZBEKISTAN
Moynoq
ARAL SEA
Turkmenbashi
Ashgabat
TURKMENISTAN

Bishkek
KYRGYZSTAN
Osh
Yining

Kyzyl

Oral
Atyrau
Ural
Aktau

CASPIAN SEA

Tehran

NORTH AMERICA

ATLANTIC OCEAN
NORTH

Greenwich Meridian

EUROPE

RUSSIA
(European area)

BLACK SEA

TURKEY
(Asian area)
TURKEY
(European area)

Ankara
Adana
Aleppo
SYRIA
Damascus

GEORGIA
Tbilisi
ARMENIA
Yerevan
AZERBAIJAN
Baku
Tabriz
Mosul
IRAQ
Baghdad

CYPRUS
Nicosia
LEBANON
Beirut
ISRAEL
Jerusalem
JORDAN

MEDITERRANEAN SEA

30°
40°
50°
40°
30°
40°

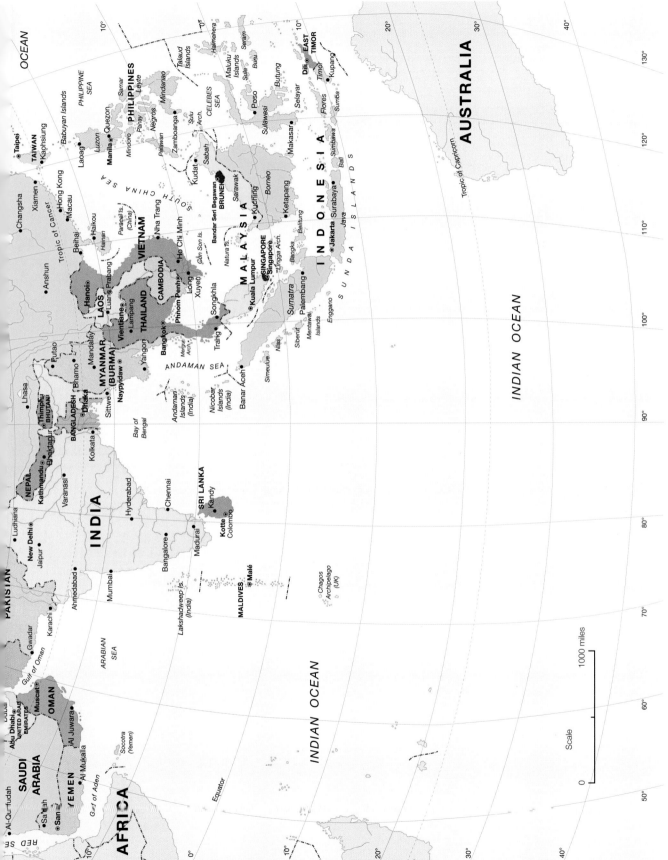

OCEAN

10°

PHILIPPINE
SEA

PHILIPPINES

Babuyan Islands

Samar

TAIWAN

Taipei

Kaohsiung

Laoag

Luzon

Quezon

Manila

Mindoro

Panay

Leyte

Negros

Mindanao

Sulu
Arch.

Zamboanga

Palawan

Talaud
Islands

Halmahera

Seram

Maluku
Islands

Sula

Buru

Butung

CELEBES
SEA

Poso

Sulawesi

Makasar

Selayar

Sumba

Flores

Sumbawa

EAST
TIMOR

Dili

Timor

Kupang

20°

30°

AUSTRALIA

Tropic of Capricorn

Changsha

Xiamen

Hong Kong

Macau

Beihai

Haikou

Tropic of Cancer

Anshun

Hainan

SOUTH CHINA SEA

Paracel Is.
(China)

Nha Trang

Ho Chi Minh

VIETNAM

Gdn Son Is.

Natura Is.

Kudat

Sabah

Kuching

BRUNEI

Bandar Seri Begawan

Sarawak

Borneo

Ketapang

Kuala Lumpur

SINGAPORE

Singapore

MALAYSIA

Bali

Ketapang

Belitung

Java

Bangka

INDONESIA

Jakarta

Surabaya

S U N D A   I S L A N D S

130°

40°

120°

110°

Hanoi

LAOS

Luang Prabang

Vientiane

Lampang

THAILAND

CAMBODIA

Phnom Penh

Long
Xuyen

Bangkok

Songkhla

Trang

Sumatra

Palembang

Lingga Arch.

Mentawai
Islands

Siberut

Nias

Enggano

INDIAN OCEAN

100°

Lhasa

Thimphu

BHUTAN

Putao

Bhamo

Mandalay

MYANMAR
(BURMA)

Naypyidaw

Yangon

Sittwe

Dhaka

BANGLADESH

Bhaktapur

Kolkata

ANDAMAN SEA

Mergui
Arch.

Banar Aceh

Andaman
Islands
(India)

Nicobar
Islands
(India)

Simeulue

90°

NEPAL

Kathmandu

Varanasi

INDIA

Hyderabad

Chennai

SRI LANKA

Kandy

Kotte

Colombo

Bay of
Bengal

Ludhiana

New Delhi

Jaipur

Bangalore

Madurai

Kolkata

Lakshadweep Is.
(India)

Chagos
Archipelago
(UK)

MALDIVES

Malé

80°

70°

PAKISTAN

Ahmedabad

Mumbai

Karachi

Gwadar

ARABIAN
SEA

INDIAN OCEAN

Al-Qurʾudah

SAUDI
ARABIA

Sabah

San

YEMEN

Al Mukalla

Socotra
(Yemen)

Abu Dhabi

UNITED ARAB
EMIRATES

Dubai

Muscat

OMAN

Al Juwara

Gulf of Oman

AFRICA

Gulf of Aden

RED SEA

20°

30°

INDIAN OCEAN

Equator

Scale

1000 miles

0

60°

50°

40°

0°

10°

GEOGRAPHICAL WONDERS

Asia, the world's largest continent, has an enormous variety of landscapes. From some of the world's largest sandy deserts to crystal clear lakes and the highest summits in the world, it is truly a region of many contrasts.

Central Asia
Regions of wide desert and barren mountains dominate the landscape of Central Asia.

TURAN AND KAZAKHSTAN
DESERTIFICATION

Dry Plateau

Central Asia is a region of hills, deserts, and plateaus. In the middle of Central Asia sits the Aral Sea, the world's fourth-largest saltwater lake. Since 1960, it has shrunk by almost 75 percent because the rivers feeding it were diverted to irrigate cotton fields. Poor vegetation combined with the region's dry climate—less than 15 inches of rain a year—have contributed to the spread of a process called desertification. This is when an area of desert begins to replace land that was previously **fertile**.

CENTRAL ASIA
ALTAI MOUNTAINS

Asia Gold Range

The Altai Mountains stretch across parts of Russia, China, Mongolia, and Kazakhstan. The mountains are separated by river valleys, which contain alpine meadows. The highest point is Mount Belukha (14,783 feet), on which there are several glaciers. The region is home to many diverse species, including the snow leopard.

CHINA
YANGTZE RIVER

Three Gorges Dam

The Yangtze River is the third-longest river in the world after the Nile and the Amazon. Its source is in Tibet and it flows for 3915 miles before reaching the Yellow Sea. In the final stretch of its upper course lies the Three Gorges Dam. A feat of engineering, this dam provides hydroelectric power to several large cities.

SAUDI ARABIA
DESERT SANDS

The Empty Quarter

South of the Arabian Peninsula is the Rub' al Khali Desert. The desert is one of the largest sandy deserts in the world and includes most of Saudi Arabia and areas of Oman, the United Arab Emirates, and Yemen, covering 250,966 square miles. It is known for its extreme weather conditions, making it virtually impossible to cross.

SIBERIA
LAKE BAIKAL

SOUTH-CENTRAL ASIA
THE HIMALAYAS

The Blue Eye of Siberia

Lake Baikal is known as the Blue Eye of Siberia because its waters are so clear and blue. Containing 20 percent of the world's fresh water, the lake is 395 miles long and 5315 feet deep. In 1996, the lake became a UNESCO World Heritage Site.

Olkhon island

The island of Olkhon (below) is 282 square miles, and is the largest island of Lake Baikal in eastern Siberia. The island is covered with forests and a small steppe, in addition to its own lakes.

The Himalayas is the world's highest mountain range. It is 1516 miles long. The range includes the formidable Mount Everest, which has a summit of 29,030 feet. The elevation of this mountain system is the result of a collision between the Indian and Eurasian tectonic plates, which began about 50 million years ago. The Himalayan region has many glaciers, which provide the area with a wealth of fresh water.

A view of Lake Baikal.

ASIAN RELIEF
ASIAN LANDSCAPE IN CROSS-SECTION

Asia has incredibly varied landscapes. As this cross-section shows, there are shields, deserts, plateaus, and basins.

The weight of the Tibetan Plateau contributes to the expansion of the Earth's crust to the east and west.

The expansion of the Earth's crust has caused faults across the Tibetan Plateau.

Arabian Shield

Persian Gulf

Iran Plateau

Thar Desert

Sichuan Basin

Lake Dongting

Earth's mantle

THE HIMALAYAS

The highest peaks on Earth, rising to over 29,000 feet, are found in this Asian mountain range. The Himalayan mountain range extends across several countries, including Pakistan, India, Nepal, Bhutan, and Tibet.

10,000
The number of attempts to climb Mount Everest in the last 50 years.

HIMALAYAN ORIGINS

Inhabitants of the Heights

The inhabitants of the Himalayas belong to many different peoples who belong to different religious groups. Mongolians, who follow Buddhism, are found mainly in the north. Muslims are found in the south, east, and west, with the center of the region dominated by Hindus.

The First

On May 29, 1953, New Zealander Edmund Hillary and his guide Tenzing Norgay (below) became the first people to reach the summit of Mount Everest. It is possible that the Englishman George Mallory succeeded in 1924, but he died during the descent.

HIMALAYAN RANGE
FACT FILE

Many Chains

The Himalayas is a system composed of numerous mountain ranges.

Area covered by the chain: 236,294 square miles

Ecosystem: High mountain

Maximum altitude: Mount Everest 29,030 feet

The Nearest Town

Muzaffarabad, the capital of Azad Kashmir, Pakistan, is located at the foot of the Himalayas. On October 8, 2005, a massive earthquake destroyed much of Muzaffarabad.

Flora

Firs, junipers (below), birch, and rhododendron plants are widespread throughout the area.

Lake Tsomgo

Located at 12,402 feet above sea level, Lake Tsomgo is 25 miles from Gangtok, the capital of the state of Sikkim. Although home to a variety of fauna and flora, the lake freezes over in the winter.

From Space

This satellite image shows the Himalayas as they look from space. The mountain range can be identified by the wrinkled appearance that it gives the Earth's surface.

RECORD
The Himalayan range has ten of the 14 highest peaks on Earth.

The Sherpas

The valleys of the Himalayas are inhabited by the Sherpas. These people are used to life in the mountains, and are often used as guides and escorts by mountaineers.

Mount Everest
The snowy peaks of the Himalayas rise high above the clouds.

MOUNT FUJI

This sacred mountain of Japan is a volcano that, while inactive for more than 300 years, is not extinct. It is considered to be the most perfect volcano on Earth because of the symmetry of its cone. At the base of Mount Fuji there are lakes, plateaus, waterfalls, and caves.

Blue and White

The blue and white flycatcher is a migratory bird. It breeds in Japan, Korea, and parts of China and Russia.

Spring

It is said to be spring in Japan when the cherry blossom tree comes into bloom.

TEMPERATURE
The lowest temperature ever recorded at Mount Fuji was -36 °F in February 1981.

Mount Fuji
Panoramic view of the volcano, the city Fujiyoshida, and Lake Kawaguchi.

Lake Kawaguchi
This lake is very famous because it reflects the north face of Mount Fuji like a mirror.

Sea of Trees

The forest *Aokigahara Jukai*, or Sea of Trees, is found on the ruins left by an eruption that took place in AD 864.

From Tokyo

In this aerial view of Tokyo, you can see Mount Fuji, a symbol of Japan, in the background.

Technical Details of Mount Fuji

Mount Fuji is located in central Japan, west of the capital Tokyo. It is an active volcano, but with little risk of eruption.

1 Location:
Honshu Island

2 Type:
Active stratovolcano

3 Maximum altitude:
12,388 feet

Icy summit

The summit of Mount Fuji very seldom reaches above 32 °F.

Sacred Spot

For centuries, Mount Fuji was considered so sacred that only monks and religious pilgrims climbed it. Until 1872, women were not allowed to climb it.

HISTORY
THREE ERUPTIONS

Mount Fuji

There have been three major eruptions of Mount Fuji, with each one adding to the shape and size of the volcano:

700,000 years ago: Komitake eruption. Its summit today overlooks the eastern slope of Fuji.

100,000 years ago: several eruptions of the Old Fuji. This was then covered by several more eruptions.

December 1707: the last eruption.

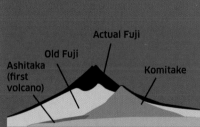

Actual Fuji

Old Fuji

Ashitaka (first volcano)

Komitake

TOURIST INFORMATION

Shiraito Falls

Although this waterfall has a drop of only about 66 feet, it is a Japanese national monument and is sacred to the Japanese. The falls are surrounded by trees, making them an attractive tourist destination.

THE MONSOON

Monsoons are seasonal winds that bring rains. They govern the life and economy of one of the most densely populated regions of the world. The monsoon season begins with heavy rains, marking the end of the dry winter. Although people welcome the end of the winter, the monsoons can cause devastating floods that can destroy crops and homes.

ORIGIN
The word monsoon comes from the Arabic "mawsim," which means "season."

Benefits from Floods

Although the locals fear the flooding, the mud left by it increases soil fertility and ensures the health of future crops.

Crops in Oman

If monsoons do not destroy homes, they are welcomed by farmers because they make the soil more fertile, which leads to better crops.

Help from Other Countries

The devastating floods of 2010 left Pakistan reliant on help from other countries. Here, an observer in a military plane examines the scene of the floods.

2400

The number of deaths that occurred during the 2008 monsoon season.

Torrential Rains

In Vietnam, in September 2009, torrential rains left 300 people homeless. Eight people were killed in the torrential rains.

India Underwater
In India, scenes like this are common during the monsoon season, which lasts from June to September.

Overflowing Rivers

Rivers that join the mighty Ganges and the Brahmaputra in Bangladesh can be affected greatly by flooding rains, which devastate crops and property, and cause landslides.

HOW IT HAPPENS
MONSOON

Temperature Differences

Monsoons are seasonal winds that vary in direction according to the season. The winter monsoon is a cold wind blowing from the continent to the ocean. The summer monsoon blows from the Indian Ocean and South China Sea into Asia, dragging with it warm and humid air. This wind crashes into the high mountains and causes heavy rains between April and October. In recent years, as a result of global warming and climate change, the monsoons have grown in intensity.

ASIAN MONSOONS
PAKISTAN-LADAKH-CHINA-KOREA

Devastation in 2010

Floods in Asia devastated large areas. In Pakistan, more than 300,000 homes were damaged or destroyed. In the region of Ladakh, India, at least 185 people died. In China, there were more than 700 deaths, and in North Korea, 800,000 people had to leave their homes.

Disaster in Pakistan
This aerial view shows the 2010 flooding in Muzaffargarh, southern Punjab, Pakistan. Around 14 million people lost their homes in the flood.

THE GANGES RIVER

The Ganges River has its source in the Himalayas, at 12,769 feet. Along its 1557 miles course, it travels through mountains and plains to eventually empty into the Bay of Bengal. Civilizations have flourished on its banks, and today, cities, fertile rice paddies, and temples are found along its banks.

City of 1000 temples

The Vishwanath temple is the holiest in Varanasi. Dedicated to the god Shiva, it is covered with 1653 pounds of gold.

GANGES BASIN
FACT FILE

Symbol of Culture

The Ganges River is sacred to those who follow Hinduism. It also provides millions of people with fresh water.

Catchment area:
563,584 miles

Source of the river:
Gomukh at the mouth of Gangotri Glacier in the Himalayas

Length: 1557 miles

BELIEFS
RELIGIOUS CUSTOMS

The River is a Goddess

For Hindus, the Ganges is personified as the goddess Ganga. Hindus believe it is important for them to bathe in the river and for the ashes of their deceased loved ones to be scattered on its waters.

The Sacred River

The Ganges is sacred to followers of the Hindu religion. Its followers believe that the water of the river will save their souls. When Hindus die, they are **cremated** and their ashes are scattered in the river.

Varanasi, India
The city, seen from the river.

Contamination

Millions of people bathe in the Ganges River. All kinds of bacteria, sewage, and remains of cremations are found in the river, making it a source of contamination.

264 million

The number of gallons of sewage found along the course of the river.

140 MILLION
There are 140 million people living in the Ganges Delta.

Suspension Bridges

There are several bridges across the Ganges, including the Lakshman Jhula (which is older) and the Ram Jhula suspension bridges. They are designed only for pedestrians, but cyclists sometimes use them.

Calcutta (Kolkata)

With over 14 million inhabitants, Calcutta is one of the largest cities along the Ganges. During the colonial era, Great Britain ruled India. This building, dating from 1921, commemorates the British queen, Victoria.

ANIMALS OF THE GOBI DESERT

The Gobi Desert in northern China and southern Mongolia is extremely dry, especially during the winter. Extraordinary fossils have been found in the desert, which is home to camels, donkeys, wild horses, birds, and reptiles.

A COLD PLACE
The Gobi Desert is cold and there is often frost on the dunes.

Small Gobi

In the area of Small Gobi (*Alashan*) in Mongolia, migratory birds build their nests in small shrubs.

Gobi bear

Persian gazelle

Bactrian camel

Asiatic wild ass

Mongolian cricket

Scorpion

Camel spider

Long-eared hedgehog   Long-eared jerboa   Mongolian gerbil

Powerful Legs

The gerbil is active at night to avoid the high daytime temperatures. Gerbils use their strong hind legs and tails to leap in search of food, such as seeds.

SPECIAL ANIMALS OF THE GOBI DESERT

Two-Humped Camels
Bactrian camels have two humps. They have adapted to the desert by growing a special coat, which helps them to withstand the extreme desert temperatures. In summer, it can reach more than 140 °F, but in winter, the temperature is often below 32 °F.

Herbivorous Desert
Altai Nature Reserve is home to Persian gazelles (below), brown bears, wild horses, and donkeys. The Persian gazelle can run quickly and cover up to 19 miles a day during winter. In the summer heat, they cover only 0.6-1.9 miles a day.

Fossils of the Gobi
The first fossils found in the Gobi were skulls of lizards and small mammals. Nests and fossilized eggs of dinosaurs have also been found. These fossils have helped scientists to understand how dinosaurs lived.

Golden eagle

Marsh warbler

500,000
The area in square miles occupied by the Gobi Desert.

Wild Horses
The wild horses of the Gobi are known to have existed for 20,000 years.

Mongolian wild horse

Tatar sand boa

Gobi gecko

Frog-eyed gecko

Boa Constrictors
Tatar sand boas are found in the Gobi Desert. These snakes hunt and kill their prey by squeezing it until it suffocates. Once the prey is dead, the snake then swallows it whole.

POPULATION AND ECONOMY

Although Asia has more people than any other continent, its population is not evenly distributed. Large uninhabited areas contrast with some of the most densely populated areas on the planet. The economy has huge inequalities. There are massive contrasts between the rich oil-producing and industrialized countries, and the poverty of the countries in the central region.

Tokyo, Japan
A crowd of people on one of its streets.

POPULATIONS
THE MOST POPULATED

Beijing, China
China's capital city, Beijing, is home to about 19.6 million people. Among its attractions are the palaces of the Forbidden City and part of the Great Wall of China.

Calcutta (Kolkata), India
The state capital of West Bengal, Calcutta has an urban area that is home to over 14 million people. Its official name is Kolkata, and until 1911, it was the capital of India.

Tourism
Asia has many places for visitors to see and tourism contributes handsomely to the economy. These camels are taking tourists to the ruins of Petra in Jordan.

Rice Paddies
Many Asian people still live in rural communities. Rice is the main agricultural product in Thailand. Rice grown there is exported around the world.

Rajasthan, India Public transportation can be extremely overcrowded in India.

REGIONAL CONTRASTS
INFRASTRUCTURE

Transportation

In richer Asian countries, with growing or developed economies, transportation is highly developed. China has large airports and rail systems. However, in less economically developed countries, transportation is poor. For example, in large parts of India transportation is scarce and unreliable.

Chinese wings China Southern Airlines is the leading airline in Asia. Elephants are often used as transportation in India.

Kuwait Oil has made Kuwait one of the richest countries in the Arabian Peninsula.

HUMAN RIGHTS
CHILDREN

Poverty

Afghanistan, Bangladesh, Cambodia, and Laos are some of the poorest countries in Asia. With little economic development, people in these countries have a shorter than average life expectancy. In India and Southeast Asia, more than 30 million children are subjected to slave labor in exchange for food.

PANORAMA
LOCAL VERSUS EXPORT

Industry in Asia

China and Japan are seen as industrial powers. Many goods are made in China and Japan and exported to the West. While there is massive industrialization in parts of Asia, local industries, such as handmade textiles, are still important to some countries in Asia.

LANGUAGES AND PEOPLE

The size and diversity of the vast Asian continent mean that the people who live there are extremely varied. There are dozens of ethnic groups on the continent, and most groups speak their own language.

Hangul

North and South Korea have the same alphabet, called the Hangul. It is made up of 24 consonants and vowels.

Religions

Islam, Buddhism, and Hinduism are the main religions practiced by the people of Asia.

MOST SPOKEN
Mandarin Chinese is one of the most widely-spoken languages in the world.

Monks reading religious texts in Tibet.

Paper and Printing
Paper was invented in China in AD 104. Later, in the eleventh century, the Chinese were the first people to use a printing press.

Hebrew
The ancient language of Hebrew died in the first century AD. Nearly 2000 years later, it was revived and is spoken by almost all Israelis.

A COMPLEX HISTORY

Ancient Civilizations

Some of the oldest civilizations in the world flourished in Asia. For example:

1 **Sumer (3200–2300 BC):** This civilization grew in today's Iraq. The Sumerians developed writing and mathematics.

2 **China (united from 221 BC):** The Chinese Empire flourished until 1912.

3 **Harappa (2600–1800 BC):** In the northwest of India, they developed a system of writing.

4 **Persia (550 BC):** The Persian Empire was centered around present-day Iran.

Islamic Empires

After the rise of Islam, various empires formed:

1 **AD 630:** The tribes of the Arabian Peninsula were united in one state, which later expanded to include Syria, Palestine, and Africa.

2 **1200–1300:** The Mongols of Central Asia started to follow Islam and formed an empire that included China and India.

3 **1300:** West Asian Turks created the Ottoman Empire, which controlled a large area until 1923.

European Colonization

From the fifteenth century, the Portuguese began to trade and settle in parts of southern Asia. From the following century, the Dutch, English, and French controlled trading posts and entire countries, such as India and Indonesia.

ETHNIC GROUPS
DIFFERENT LANGUAGES

MYANMAR
KAYAN

Long-Necked Women

Women of the Kayan people lengthen their necks by wearing long collars. With a population of just 130,000, the Kayan are one of Myanmar's ethnic minorities.

CHINA–VIETNAM–MYANMAR
MIAO

Living in the Mountains

There are 7 million Miao people. They are found in the mountain regions of China, Vietnam, and Myanmar. Their language is spoken in much of Southeast Asia.

FROM ASIA TO THE WORLD
ROMA

Mother and Daughter

The Roma can be traced back to northwestern India to the states of Punjab, Gujarat, Rajasthan, and Sindh (now Pakistan). Members of this group speak Romany.

INDIA
TODA

Pastoral People

Speaking a Dravidian language, this group lives in the Nilgiri Hills in southern India. They are shepherds and live in thatched houses built on wooden frames.

THE MONGOLS

Descended from the tribes led by Genghis Khan, the leader who conquered most of Eurasia in the early thirteenth century, the Mongols still live in the steppes of Asia, just as their ancestors did. Their lifestyle also remains largely unchanged and is still centered around their horses and grazing cattle.

FROM ASIA
THE BERING STRAIT

Across Continents
Around 15,000–20,000 years ago, the Earth was approaching the end of the last glacial period. At that time, a small group of people ventured into northeastern Asia. They were probably in pursuit of game to hunt. The people crossed the Bering Strait, where the sea level was most likely lower than it is today. They had left Asia and arrived on the continent of North America in Alaska. The people eventually made North America their home.

A LARGE FAMILY

Asian and North American

Most scientists believe that the ancient Asians (their descendants are pictured below) who now inhabit southern Siberia are related to today's Native Americans.

Lunar New Year
Mongolians celebrate New Year according to the old **lunar calendar**. The festival is celebrated for three days in late January. People entertain guests and cook special food.

Traditional Houses

Many Mongolians still live in large tents called yurts. The tents are easily transportable and suit the Mongolians' nomadic way of life.

Nomadic Economy

Cattle give the Mongolians food in the form of meat and milk, transportation, and skins. Families travel great distances to find food for their cattle.

Hunting
A nomad on the steppes of Mongolia.

Culture

There are around 7–7.5 million Mongolians. Traditionally, they were hunters. Today, hunting is still an important part of their lives. They have a great spirit of cooperation and are usually very friendly with each other.

Beliefs

The Mongolian people have built shrines from rocks or wood, called oboo, in which they believe local spirits and gods live. Shrines usually face south or southeast.

Mongolian Song and Dance

Mongolians perform the *tsam*—a traditional masked dance to exorcize evil spirits. Mongolians play music on a variety of instruments and sing traditional songs.

THE TAJ MAHAL

The Taj Mahal is a beautiful mausoleum, or tomb, next to the Yamuna River in the Indian city of Agra. It was built in the seventeenth century by the Mogul emperor Shah Jahan to honor his wife, Mumtaz Mahal, who had died in childbirth. They are now both buried in this sparkling mausoleum built of white marble with precious stones laid into it.

LIGHT
The precious stones embedded in the marble sparkle in the light, giving color to the marble.

THE TAJ MAHAL
FACT FILE

Location:
Agra, India

Type
Mausoleum

Built:
Between 1631 and 1654

Commissioned by:
Emperor Shah Jahan, the Mogul Dynasty

Height:
243 feet

Construction:
43 types of marble and precious stones (turquoise, agate, lapis, coral, jade, and malachite)

Symmetry
The palace was located at the bottom of the field, behind the fountains and gardens. This meant that nothing obstructed the view of the **mausoleum.**

1. Royal tomb
2. Mosque
3. Jawab
4. Canal
5. Palace gardens
6. Grand entrance

TAJ MAHAL **DETAILS**

Arches
The arches of each doorway give depth to the structure and reflect sunlight.

Lattices
Filigree railings surround the area of the royal tombs.

Borders
Drawing and verses from the Koran have been used to add decoration.

Onion-shaped dome
Domes of this shape are typical of Islamic architecture.

Minarets

Plinth
The mausoleum sits on a plinth. It adds height to the building, making it look more impressive.

Minarets
The tomb is surrounded by four towers, or minarets, one at each corner of the base. Faithful Muslims are called to prayer from the minarets.

22
The number of small domes symbolize the years of work.

Gardens
The gardens are divided into 16 sections, with many beds of flowers, raised paths, rows of trees, fountains, streams, and wide ponds. The water reflects the majestic palace.

DETAIL
THE TOMBS

Features
Made of marble decorated with rhinestones, the tombs are found in the main building. They are decorated by a ring of lotus flowers. This decoration is repeated on each minaret.

Shah Jahan

Mumtaz Mahal

Burial Chamber
The tombs of the couple are found in the central hall of the mausoleum.

BEIJING

The People's Republic of China's capital city, Beijing, is one of the world's most densely populated cities. The city is a mix of the ultramodern and the ancient, with skyscrapers and office towers sitting alongside ancient palaces, temples, and plazas.

Dashalar
A view of this bustling shopping center, just south of Tiananmen Square.

Country	China
Area	6487 sq mi
Population	19,612,000
Density	3023 people/sq mi

CITY ICONS

Temple of Heaven

This round temple complex is typical of the buildings of the Ming Dynasty. Each morning in the temple grounds, people practice t'ai chi and qigong.

Tiananmen Square

Surrounded by public buildings, this is a large square in the center of Beijing. It is the third largest public square in the world and has been the site of many events in Chinese history.

Dragon
The dragon is a symbol of force and power in Chinese culture.

SHOPPING
In this shopping avenue, shoppers can find everything, from modern jewelry and designer clothes, to traditional healers and medicines.

Entrance to Dashalar
Dashalar is a shopping avenue with more than 580 years of history. This bustling area gives an indication of what the ancient city of Beijing was like.

Transportation

The city has a wide range of public transportation that includes a subway, trains, buses, trams, and airplanes. The image on the left shows Beijing Central Station.

Beijing National Stadium

The 2008 Olympic Stadium has been nicknamed the "bird's nest" because of the intricate network of steel on its outside. The stadium is 1083 feet long, 722 feet wide, and 226 feet high.

CULTURAL EXPRESSIONS

National Grand Theater

This building was designed by Paul Andreu and resembles an egg cut in half. The lagoon it rests on reflects the other half to make a complete oval. The theater offers drama, dance, and opera.

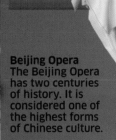

Beijing Opera
The Beijing Opera has two centuries of history. It is considered one of the highest forms of Chinese culture.

Population

Including the greater metropolitan area, the Beijing population is expected to reach 20 million by 2020.

THE FORBIDDEN CITY

Building of the Forbidden City in Beijing, China, began in 1406 during the Ming Dynasty. The city, with nearly 1000 buildings, took 14 years to complete. It was home to 24 emperors.

View of the museum Beijing, China.

Roofs
Pottery figurines of dragons and winged lions protect the Forbidden City from evil spirits.

THE FORBIDDEN CITY
FACT FILE

Date of construction:
1406–1420

Location:
Beijing, China

Features:
Covering 861,110 square feet, the city is surrounded by a moat that is 20 feet deep. Its thick walls are capable of withstanding gunfire.

Sahumadores

The palaces and courtyards had beautiful perfume burners, which spread a cloud of scent during ceremonies.

EXTREME SECURITY

Defense of the City

In addition to its thick walls and surrounding moat, the city has watchtowers at each of its corners. It was called Forbidden City, because no one was allowed to enter or leave the city without permission from the emperor.

Ornamentation
Most of the buildings were built of wood. The ceilings have fine woodworked details on their eaves and numerous decorative pieces.

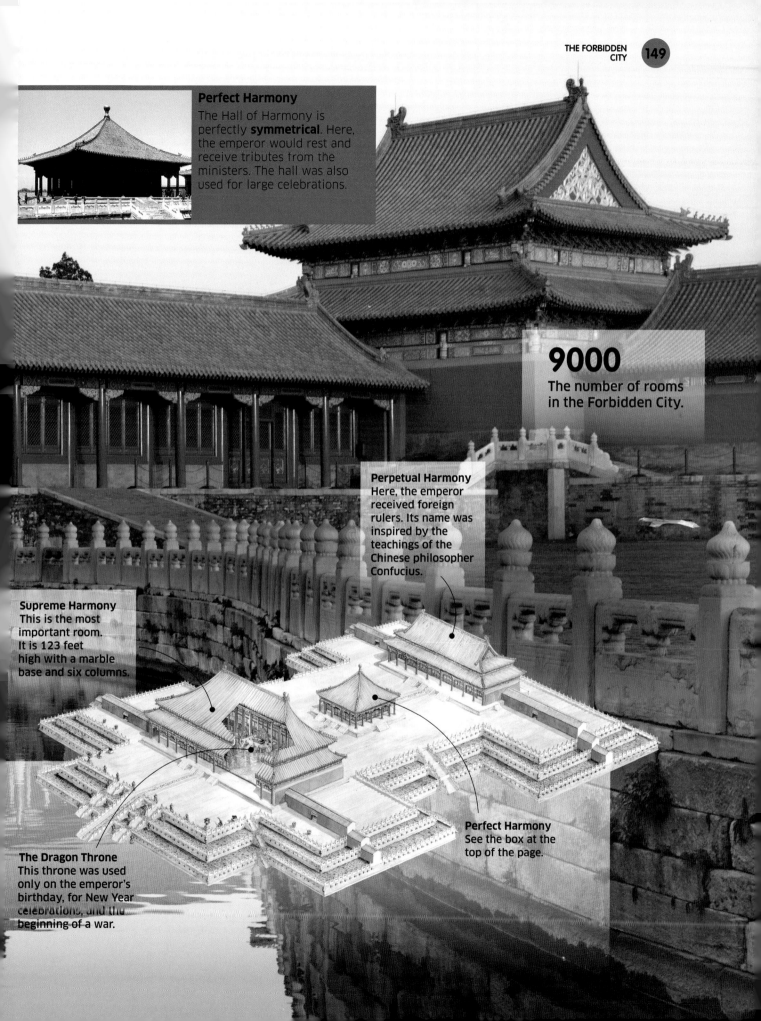

Perfect Harmony

The Hall of Harmony is perfectly **symmetrical**. Here, the emperor would rest and receive tributes from the ministers. The hall was also used for large celebrations.

9000

The number of rooms in the Forbidden City.

Perpetual Harmony

Here, the emperor received foreign rulers. Its name was inspired by the teachings of the Chinese philosopher Confucius.

Supreme Harmony

This is the most important room. It is 123 feet high with a marble base and six columns.

The Dragon Throne

This throne was used only on the emperor's birthday, for New Year celebrations, and the beginning of a war.

Perfect Harmony

See the box at the top of the page.

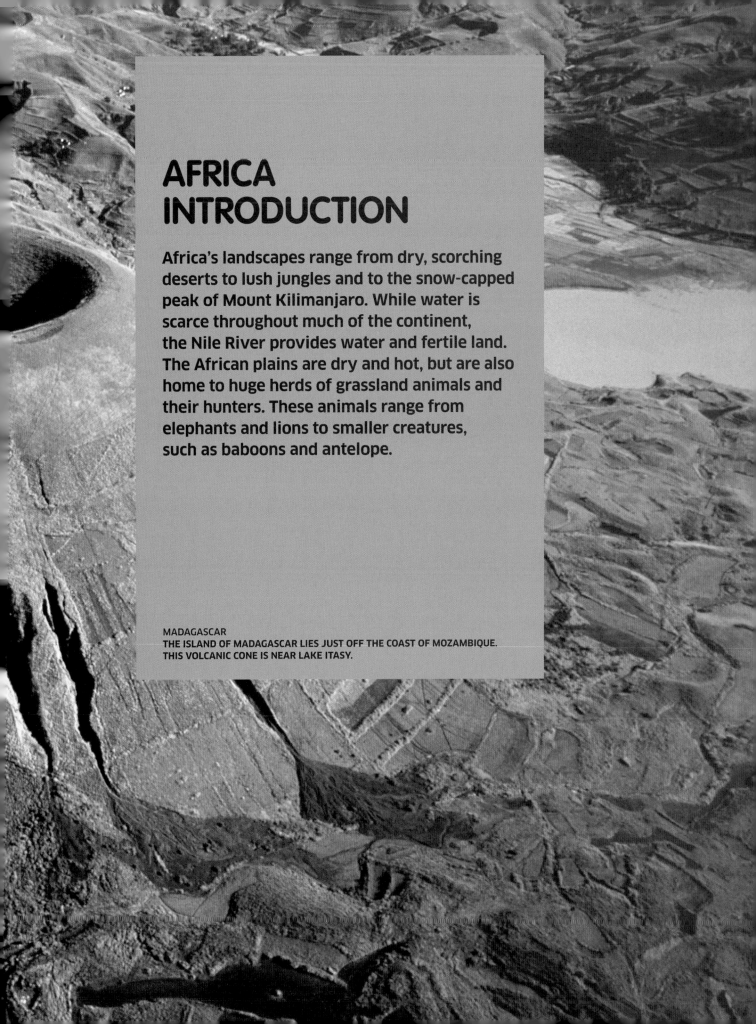

AFRICA INTRODUCTION

Africa's landscapes range from dry, scorching deserts to lush jungles and to the snow-capped peak of Mount Kilimanjaro. While water is scarce throughout much of the continent, the Nile River provides water and fertile land. The African plains are dry and hot, but are also home to huge herds of grassland animals and their hunters. These animals range from elephants and lions to smaller creatures, such as baboons and antelope.

MADAGASCAR
THE ISLAND OF MADAGASCAR LIES JUST OFF THE COAST OF MOZAMBIQUE.
THIS VOLCANIC CONE IS NEAR LAKE ITASY.

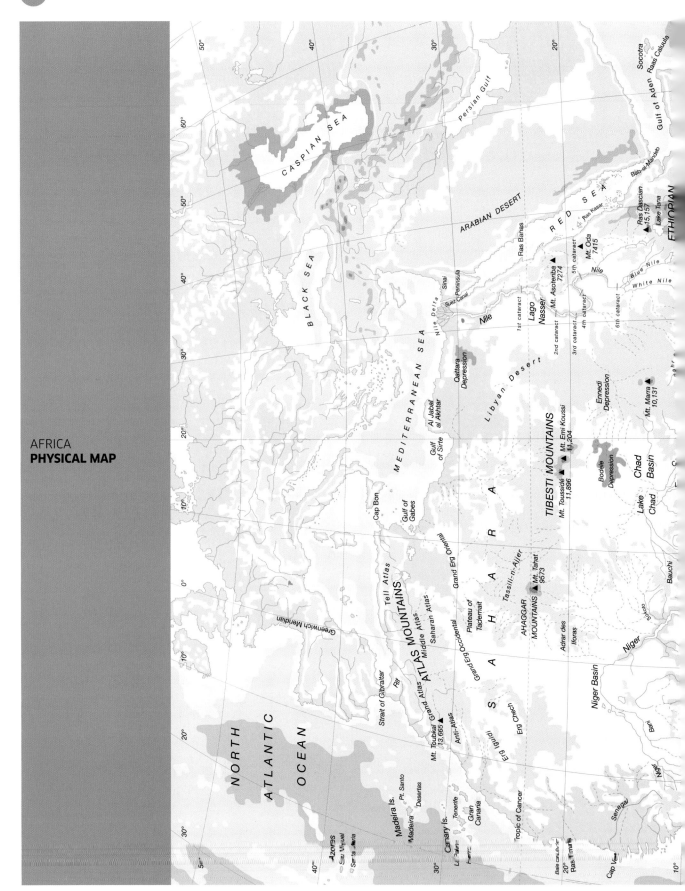

AFRICA
PHYSICAL MAP

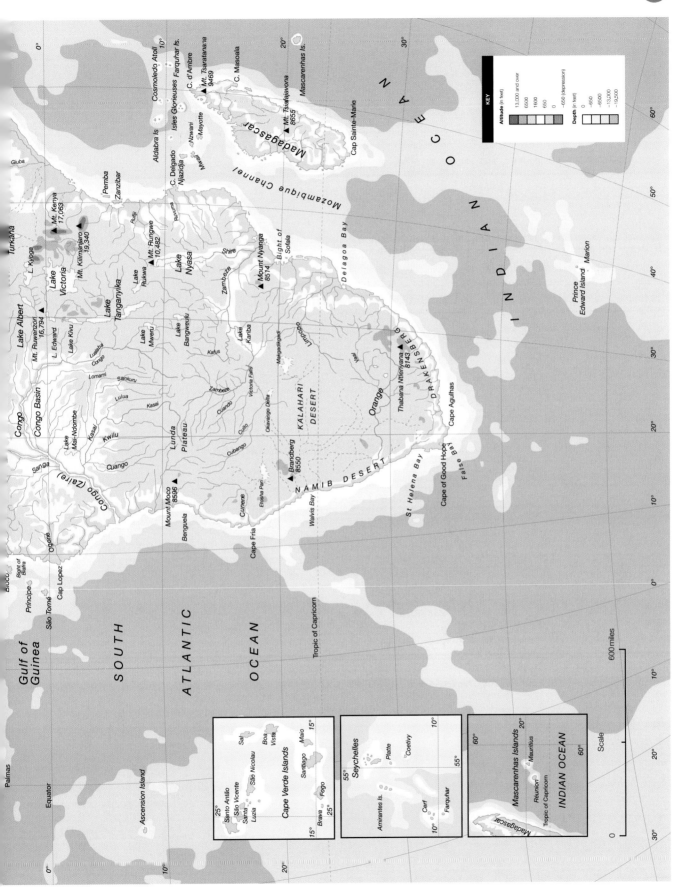

KEY

Altitude (in feet)

13,000 and over
6500
1600
650
0
−650 (depression)

Depth (in feet)

0
−650
−6500
−13,000
−19,500

INDIAN OCEAN

SOUTH ATLANTIC OCEAN

Gulf of Guinea

Congo Basin

Congo (Zaire)

KALAHARI DESERT

NAMIB DESERT

DRAKENSBERG

Lake Victoria

Lake Tanganyika

Lake Nyasa

Mozambique Channel

Madagascar

Mt. Kilimanjaro 19,340

Mt. Kenya 17,063

Mt. Ruwenzori 16,794

Mt. Rungwe 10,482

Mount Nyanga 8514

Thabana Ntlenyana 8143

Mount Moco 8596

Brandberg 8550

Mt. Tsaratanana 9469

Mt. Tsiafajavona 8655

Cape Verde Islands

Seychelles

Mascarenhas Islands
INDIAN OCEAN

Scale
600 miles

Equator

Tropic of Capricorn

Cape of Good Hope
Cape Agulhas

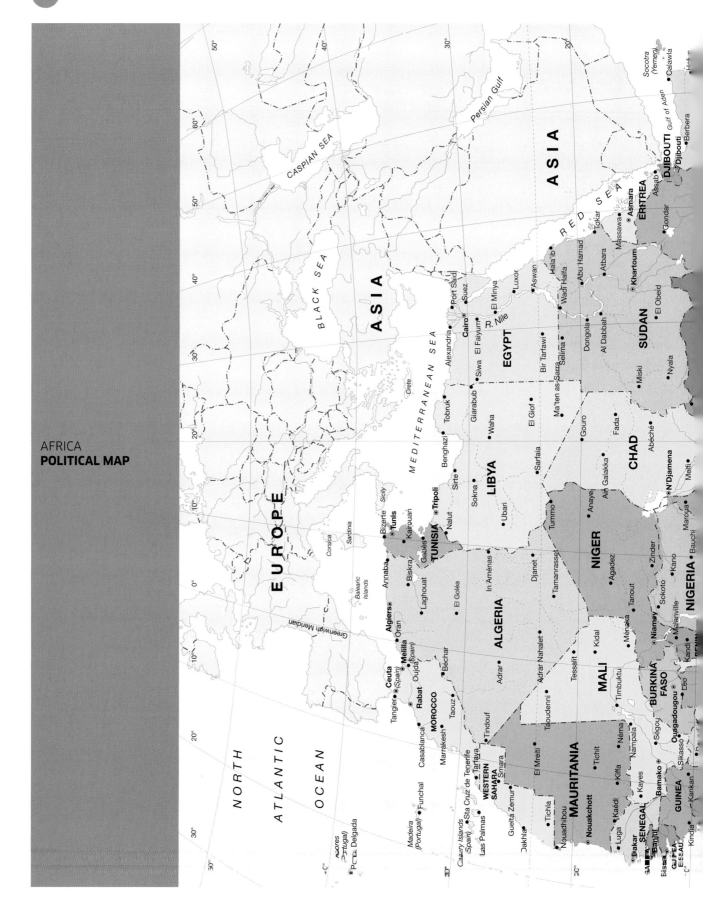

AFRICA
POLITICAL MAP

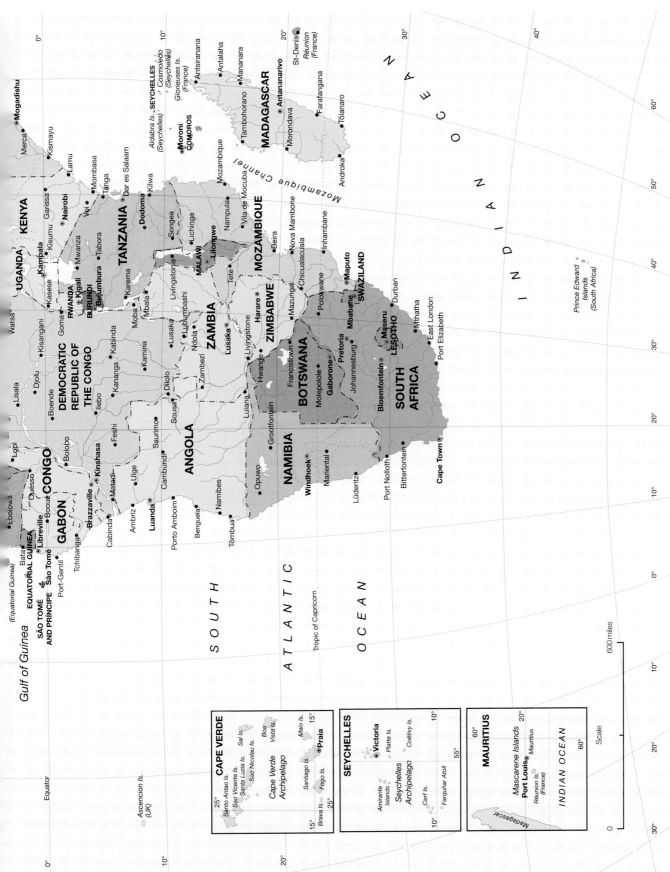

GEOGRAPHICAL WONDERS

As a result of wind and water erosion, plateaus dominate the African landscape. The northern region is home to the Atlas Mountains. In the eastern region, the Great Rift Valley divides Africa from north to south.

A caravan of camels crossing the Sahara

SAHARA
THE WORLD'S LARGEST DESERT

Temperature

The Sahara is the world's biggest desert extending nearly 3.47 million square miles. Mountains, including the Ahaggar Mountains in southern Algeria (which have peaks of up to 9843 feet high), interrupt the desert landscape. The difference in temperature varies greatly between day and night. During the day, the temperature can reach above 122 °F; but at night it can drop to 32 °F.

TUNISIA–ALGERIA–MOROCCO
MOUNTAIN RANGES

Atlas Mountains

With peaks reaching more than 13,123 feet, the Atlas Mountains in North Africa feature some of the highest peaks on the continent. The mountains run from east to west over 1300 miles and cross three countries.

ZAMBIA–ZIMBABWE
ZAMBEZI RIVER

Kariba Dam

In Africa, there are more than 1200 dams. Like the Kariba Dam, most of them were built as a solution to problems such as drought. Building these dams has caused serious damage to ecosystems and has led to a massive displacement of people.

DJIBOUTI–MOZAMBIQUE
GEOLOGICAL FRACTURE

Rift Valley

The Great Rift Valley is one of Africa's most important geographical features. It was formed 20–25 million years ago, when the Earth's crust broke along a stretch of weakness. It extends from western Asia to southeastern Africa.

KENYA
VOLCANIC MOUNTAINS

The Last Glaciers

There are only three glaciers left in Africa: Mount Kilimanjaro, Mount Kenya (left), which are both of volcanic origin, and Rwenzori Mountains. With the rapid increase in global warming, these glaciers are in serious danger of disappearing.

Old Volcano

Mount Kenya was covered by ice for thousands of years. This has resulted in a badly eroded hillside and numerous valleys. It is now made up of 11 small glaciers.

Mount Kilimanjaro
An icy summit contrasts with the surrounding landscape.

ZAMBIA–ZIMBABWE
VICTORIA FALLS

Waterfalls

The Victoria Falls are located on the border between Zambia and Zimbabwe. The Falls are neither the world's highest nor widest. However, their height of 328 feet and their width of 5577 feet combined, make them the mightiest in the world. The Falls have been declared a World Heritage Site by UNESCO.

PROFILE
THE AFRICAN CONTINENT

This cross-section, from northwest to southeast, shows the great contrasts in the continent's relief.

19,340 FT
The height of Mount Kilimanjaro, Africa's highest mountain.

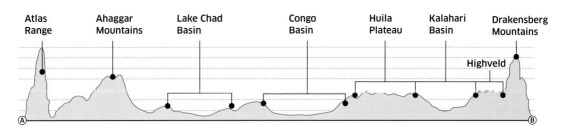

Atlas Range

Ahaggar Mountains

Lake Chad Basin

Congo Basin

Huila Plateau

Kalahari Basin

Drakensberg Mountains

Highveld

A

B

MOUNT KILIMANJARO

Africa's tallest mountain is a huge volcano that rises 19,340 feet above sea level. Although Mount Kilimanjaro is only 205 miles south of the equator, its summit remains covered with a layer of **permafrost**. The last volcanic activity on the mountain was just 200 years ago.

Elephants

Elephants, buffaloe and giraffes can be found on the surrounding plains.

Glaciers

Mount Kilimanjaro's glaciers are shrinking as a result of global warming and possibly volcanic activity.

Three in One

Kilimanjaro has three craters: Kibo, Mawenzi, and Shira. Mount Meru, in the Monduli Mountains, and Ngurdoto Crater lie to the west.

CRATERS OF KILIMANJARO

Monduli Mountains · Ngurdoto Crater · Mount Meru · Shira · Kibo · Mawensi

Technical Data

Kilimanjaro is a stratovolcano located in Tanzania, East Africa.

1. **Geological system:** the Great Rift Valley which crosses from north to south.

2. **Neighboring ecosystems:** forests and meadows.

3. **Maximum altitude: Kibo Crater, 19,340 feet.**

40,000

The number of people visiting Kilimanjaro National Park each year.

Snowy peaks
An aerial view of Kilimanjaro.

A FASCINATING LANDSCAPE

POPULATION
DIFFERENT ETHNIC GROUPS

Daily Life

The Chagga, Masai, and Hadza are just three of the many ethnic groups that live near Mount Kilimanjaro. The Chagga people's livelihood depends on agriculture, and they grow bananas, yams (a type of tuber), beans, and corn. The Masai are a seminomadic tribe that lives in northern Tanzania. They roam the plains raising cattle, sheep, and goats. The Hadza (right) neither raise cattle nor do they grow crops. Instead, they forage the land as their ancestors did 10,000 years ago.

ROUTES OF ASCENT

Mountaineering and Nature

Climbers of Mount Kilimanjaro do not need specific mountaineering experience to climb to the summit successfully, but they do need to be fit and healthy. Most people who climb the mountain do so with the help of a local guide. One of the biggest challenges for climbers is the altitude, which can cause headaches and breathing difficulties. Nearly one-third of climbers fail to reach the summit. There are several routes to the summit, including Rongai, Machame, and Marangu, which is the preferred route.

THE NILE RIVER

The legendary Nile in Egypt is the longest river in Africa and also in the world. (The Amazon River in South America is the largest river by volume of water.) The course of the river's flow of water makes parts of the desert habitable. Also, along the banks of the Nile River emerged one of the most important civilizations: ancient Egypt.

ELEVEN COUNTRIES
TRAVEL

Without Borders

The Nile River runs through 11 countries: Egypt, Sudan, South Sudan, Democratic Republic of Congo, Rwanda, Uganda, Tanzania, Kenya, Ethiopia, Burundi, and Eritrea. It crosses through deserts, forests, savannas, swamps, and mountains. The Nile River Delta is one of the largest deltas in the world, and as a result of its fertile land, it is densely populated.

The Big Meeting

In the city of Khartoum, Sudan's capital, the White Nile from Uganda meets the Blue Nile, which flows from Ethiopia. These two tributaries flow together to form the Nile River.

DESCENT
From its source to its mouth, the Nile drops nearly 6562 feet.

95
The percentage of the Egyptian population that lives in the area of influence of the Nile.

4160 miles
The length of the Nile River.

Satellite image of the Nile River. Its huge delta flows into the Mediterranean.

DAMS
DIKES AND RESERVOIRS

Ecological Damage

Since the late nineteenth century, many dams and reservoirs have been built on the Nile. These dams have caused great ecological damage. An example is the Aswan High Dam, built between 1960 and 1970 in Aswan, Egypt. The dam was seen as a way to ensure a permanent supply of water and a source of hydroelectric power. By damming the Nile, several river species have disappeared and the salt levels of the Delta's water have increased greatly.

Crocodiles

The Nile crocodile is a powerful predator, capable of killing a man.

Monuments

On both sides of the Nile stand great monuments, such as Luxor, the Valley of the Kings, and the Pyramids of Giza.

FLORA AND FAUNA

Africa's rainfall is erratic and many parts of the continent experience regular droughts. Drought, together with humankind's actions, mean that many animal species, such as the gorilla and rhinoceros, are in danger of extinction.

Comoé National Park
This park lies in the Ivory Coast.

ISLAND OF MADAGASCAR
DIFFERENT SPECIES

Fossa

The fossa is found in the forests of Madagascar. Measuring from 31–35 inches long, this mammal can weight up to 22 pounds. The fossa is quick and agile, catching its prey of lemurs and birds easily.

Hands of Stone

Tsingy National Park is in the central west region of Madagascar. The park is home to various species of plant and animal, such as the lemur. The area is famous for its hard rock in the shape of needles.

Gorillas

Hunting, mining, and deforestation threaten the gorilla. Gorillas are found in forested areas, from Cameroon to the Democratic Republic of Congo.

Lemurs

The ring-tailed lemur is found in the wild only on the island of Madagascar. Lemurs feed on roots, leaves, fruits, and insects.

Zebras
There are three different species of zebra found in Africa.

Baobab

The "upside-down tree" or baobab is found in the semi-arid regions of sub-Saharan Africa. These trees can store up to 264,000 gallons of water. The people of Africa use the tree in many different ways: rope and baskets are made from the bark fiber, and the leaves and fruit are eaten. The fruit is very rich in vitamin C.

DESERT
TYPES OF VEGETATION

Palms

The desert vegetation of Africa has adapted to its environment. While shrubs, grasses, and thorny plants grow in the desert itself, fruit, cereals, and date palms flourish around oases. Date palms are especially useful to the people of the desert. Their leaves are used to provide shade and building materials for furniture, mats, and baskets. The fruit is also eaten.

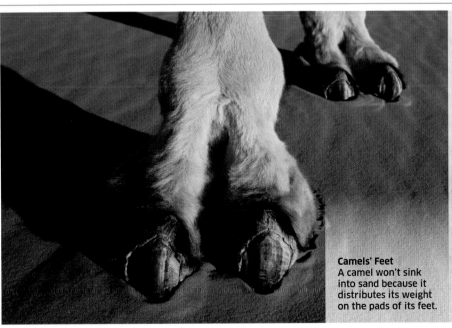

Camels' Feet
A camel won't sink into sand because it distributes its weight on the pads of its feet.

RESISTANT MAMMALS

Master of the Desert

Thanks to the camel's strength, these animals are used to carry loads across the desert as well as for farm work. They are also kept for their meat, wool, and skins.

THE OKAVANGO DELTA

This extraordinary natural environment occupies 14.8 million acres and has a rich biodiversity. After the summer rains, the Okavango River in Botswana swells, and the rate of its water flow increases. The river flows to one of the driest areas of the world: the Kalahari Desert.

6487 SQ MI

The surface area of the Okavango Delta.

HIPPO WARNING
Hippopotamuses open their mouths wide to display large fangs. They do this to intimidate their prey.

African jabiru

Hammerhead stork

Hippopotamus

African tiger fish

African pike

BETWEEN WATER AND LAND
The hippopotamus spends the daylight hours semi-submerged in water and the evening out to pasture. Hippos can eat 99 pounds of plants in one night.

PAYBACK
Hippo dung provides nutrients for the aquatic plants. These plants are then fed on by fish, birds, and crocodiles.

APPROPRIATE SUPPORT
The sitatunga antelope has open hooves that are specially adapted for treading on soft ground.

Papyrus

Sitatunga

Wattled crane

MARSHLAND
Water from heavy rains in Angola transforms arid land into fertile swamp.

Nile crocodile

ADAPTATIONS
Wetlands are home to a great range of plants and animals. Mammals, reptiles, amphibians, fish, and insects are all found in wetlands. Wetland animals are also adapted to dive into the water. For example, crocodiles have nostrils, eyes, and ears on top of their head, so they can breathe, hear, and see without leaving the water. Hippos can close their nostrils and slow their heart rate down so much that they can stay underwater for half an hour.

GIANT IN THE OKAVANGO

Elephants in the Wild
The Okavango Delta is home to many large herds of elephant. In total, there are about 30,000 elephants in the region.

The animals form herds of females and calves. The presence of elephants is easy to recognize, because they often damage trees, stripping the bark, which is left behind on the ground.

AQUATIC PLANTS
TYPICAL EXAMPLES

Papyrus and Water Sprouts
Plants growing in the wetlands live either entirely or almost entirely submerged in water. **Papyrus**, water lilies, and water sprouts are the most common plants in the habitat. Water birds often walk on the plants in search of food.

Crocodiles
The Nile crocodile is the largest crocodile in Africa. It feeds on fish, antelopes, zebras, buffaloes, and poultry.

THE AFRICAN SAVANNA

The African continent has the most extensive savanna in the world. Unlike the North American prairies, the African grasslands have shrubs and trees, such as acacias and baobabs. Many **herbivore** animals live together with their predators in this environment.

Giraffe

African elephant

African marabou

Zebra

Wildebeest

White-backed vulture

Termite

Termite mound

HERBIVORES AND PREDATORS
The savanna is home to many herbivores, grass and plant-eating animals, including buffaloes, zebras, wildebeest, elephants, rhinoceros, and giraffes. The predators found in the savanna are lions, leopards, cheetahs, and eagles. There are several different species of vulture, which are **scavengers**.

TERMITE SOCIETY
Termites are social insects like bees and ants. The members of each colony build a large nest made from their droppings, which contain sawdust. Inside the mound is a sophisticated network of tunnels to ensure the circulation of fresh air. The tunnels cannot be reached by predators.

White rhinoceros

ACACIA
The acacia tree provides herbivores, such as giraffe, with food. Its wood is also especially strong.

Lion

Scarab beetle

ANIMALS
SCAVENGERS

Hyenas

The spotted hyena is found south of the Sahara, from Senegal and the Upper Nile to the southern tip of Africa. The hyena is known for its ungainly body. It scavenges on the prey remains of the big cats, for which it competes with vultures and jackals. In addition, hyenas are highly efficient hunters. To attack their prey, they use their powerful jaws. They also hunt as a pack, allowing them to prey on larger animals, such as zebras, giraffes, and wildebeests.

Data file

Height:	28–35 inches
Weight:	88–154 pounds
Gestation period:	110 days
Number of offspring:	2

Vultures

These scavengers are distinguished by their bald heads. By not having feathers on their heads, vultures can sift through the bloody remains of a kill without their heads becoming breeding grounds for parasites and disease. Vultures can have wingspans of up to 8 feet. In addition, they are able to hover in the sky using the air currents in search of prey.

Data file

Height:	37–43 inches
Weight:	up to 18.7 pounds
Gestation period:	55 days
Number of offspring:	1

POPULATION

In Africa, the population is distributed according to each region's natural resources. For example, there are more people in the fertile coastal regions north and west of Nigeria, the Nile Valley, and the eastern plateau. In recent decades, many people in rural areas have migrated to urban cities.

Cape Town
The urban sprawl of Cape Town on the mountainous coast of South Africa.

RAPID GROWTH

Nigerian Children

The rate at which the population grows in Africa is high: the continental average is 2.3 percent each year. Lagos in Nigeria is one of Africa's most populous cities.

Dakar

The site of the current capital of Senegal, Dakar, was first colonized by Europeans in the fifteenth century. The port is in a strategic position for maritime trade with both North America and Europe. Today, it is one of the busiest ports in the world and is used to transport goods, such as chemicals, food, and tobacco, from Mali and Mauritania.

EGYPT
CAIRO

An Important City

Egypt's capital, Cairo, is located on the shores and islands of the Nile River. The city has theaters, universities, and museums. Few places combine the past and present as Cairo does. On the streets of Cairo, it is not uncommon to see carts pulled by donkeys next to expensive modern vehicles. Markets are crowded and the ringing of cell phones and public calls to prayer add to the hubbub of the markets.

REPUBLIC OF SOUTH AFRICA
JOHANNESBURG

Economic and Financial Center

Johannesburg is the largest city in South Africa, one of the continent's wealthiest countries. The wealth stems from the rich gold, diamond, and **platinum** mining industries. Johannesburg's city center is home to 3 million people, but its metropolitan area is home to more than 7 million people. The majority of the population are black South Africans (73 percent).

Kampala
A street in the old city.

UGANDA
KAMPALA

HIV and Malnutrition

The capital of Uganda, Kampala has a population of 1.6 million. The area has one of the highest rates of **HIV** infection. This reduces the productivity of families, which in turn increases the cases of malnutrition and orphaned children.

Street vendor
In Uganda, more than half the population is under 15 years old.

MOROCCO
MARRAKECH

Trade Center

The city of Marrakech was founded in 1062 by the Arabs. It became an important trading center with the rest of Africa. Marrakech was a point of arrival and departure for merchants, and the city's wealth attracted builders and craftspeople. Today, the city is known for its market, which offers a variety of goods, from traditional crafts to modern appliances.

PEOPLE AND LANGUAGES

With more than 3000 different groups of peoples in Africa, many have retained their identity by keeping their own language. Today, there are more than 2000 different languages spoken in Africa. The continent also has English, French, and Arabic-speaking countries as a result of colonial times.

Most Spoken

Arabic is one of the most widely-spoken languages in Africa. Other key languages include Swahili, Lingala, and Bambara, as well as Portuguese, English, French, and Spanish.

NOMADIC PEOPLE
In the twenty-first century, many people have held on to their own customs, such as the nomadic Tuareg from the north.

Education
Often, classes are held outside, such as this one in Makpandu, Sudan.

Papyrus

The papyrus plant that grows in the Nile Valley was used by ancient Egyptians to make paper. This invention means we now know about written history.

Muslims

After their conquests of the seventh century, the Arabs brought Islam to the territories of North Africa.

CULTURAL ISSUES
DIFFERENT HISTORIES

Four Groups

Experts have divided the many African languages into four main families:

1. **Afro-Asian (Arabic, Berber)**
2. **Niger-Congo (Bantu, Zulu)**
3. **Nilo-Saharan (Fur, Songhai)**
4. **Khoisan (Khoi, San)**

Religions

There is a great variety of religions on the continent. Often, a religion blends two or more of these. For example:

1. **Animism**
2. **Polytheism**
3. **Islam**
4. **Christianity**

Great Kingdoms

Many different civilizations formed powerful kingdoms that flourished on the continent. For example:

1. **Egypt (3000–332 BC)**
2. **Ghana (800–1235)**
3. **Mali (1200–1600)**
4. **Benin (1500–1600)**
5. **Northern Arab Caliphates (641–1171)**

European Colonization

From 1884 to 1885, the European powers divided most of the continent into colonies. Although Spain, Germany, and Belgium had their own colonies, most countries were colonized by:

1. **France**
2. **Great Britain**
3. **Portugal**

VARIETY
AFRICAN TRIBES

CAMEROON–CONGO–ANGOLA
BANTU

Villagers

A variety of peoples who speak Bantu languages have held on to their traditional customs and base their economy on agriculture.

CONGO
PYGMIES

Gatherers

Large populations of pygmy, or very small, people are found in the forested areas of the Congo. These people are gatherers.

KENYA–TANZANIA
MASAI

Semi-Nomadic People

The life of the Masai revolves around raising cattle, sheep and goats. There are around 900,000 Masai on the continent.

DESERTS
BEDOUIN

Nomadic Herders

The Bedouins of North Africa are Muslim and speak several dialects of Arabic.

THE SAN PEOPLE

The San, or Bushmen, are the native people of southern Africa. Originally, they were found in South Africa, Zimbabwe, Lesotho, Mozambique, Swaziland, Botswana, Namibia, and Angola. These people were traditionally hunter-gatherers, and today, their dwindling tribe is found mainly in the Kalahari Desert.

OUR PAST
WHAT MODERN SCIENCE TELLS US

Africa: Starting Point

According to modern genetic studies, the San are the oldest living tribe. It is believed that they are one of the original tribes from whom all others evolved. The San are typically short people with light skin and curly hair. A typical member of the San tribe has a thick layer of skin over the eyes, called the epicanthic fold, which is also characteristic of the peoples of the East.

USING SOUND TO COMMUNICATE

Peculiarity

The language spoken by the San is characterized by its clicking or popping sounds, a feature found in the languages of other groups of ancient African tribes.

Their Dress

San men wear a triangular loincloth, with the tip passed between their legs. The women wear an apron, a hanging square in front of a belt. They also wear cloaks over their shoulders.

Kalahari Desert

The San are found in the dry Kalahari Desert. They obtain food by hunting animals and gathering plants. Some San have found work as shepherds.

Water Collection

To survive, the San have to be able to find water. They suck water from plant roots and empty ostrich eggs. This image (left) shows an ostrich egg next to a hen's egg.

Hunters

San men hunt alone or with their children, using bows and arrows. Their arrows are dipped in poison, which they get from poisonous snakes.

Kalahari Desert
San children and a woman sit around a campfire.

Tradition of Fire

San people would traditionally light a fire by turning a stick on soft wood.

Houses

San shelters are made by the women wherever there is vegetation. When their food supply runs out, the group will move to another area.

Art

San cave paintings are some of the oldest in the world. Their paintings often tell a hunting story. This example (left) is found in a cave in Murewa, Zimbabwe.

ECONOMIC RESOURCES

Africa may often appear to lack wealth. However, its natural resources offer huge potential wealth. The continent has the greatest sources of precious stones and metals in the world. South Africa has some of the richest companies and industries on the continent.

Marrakech market
Every day, thousands of people visit the market, filled with crafts and other products.

AFRICAN ART
DIFFERENT TRADITIONS

Features

Because of very different traditions, African art often reflects its mixed heritage. It includes wooden sculptures, masks, and crafts in metal and other materials.

Lamp
A traditional North African lamp made from brass and stained glass.

KENYA
FARMING

Subsistence and Export

There are two types of farming on the African continent. The first is called subsistence farming. Here, a farmer will work small areas of land, growing just enough food for the farmer and the immediate family. The second type of farming is large-scale agriculture for the export of crops. This type of farming now occupies nearly 40 percent of land that is suitable for farming. It consists of large plantations, often owned by foreign companies. The most common crops grown include cocoa, bananas, coffee, and tea.

A tea picker in Kenya.

TOURISM
SAFARIS

Most Visited

Tourism provides a great source of income for the continent. Many visitors go on safari in Kenya and Tanzania to see African wildlife in its natural habitat.

In the Sahara Goats provide a good source of food in desert areas.

Consuming Local Food

Africa has rich resources of fish. A good source of food, most fish caught is eaten locally. Only Morocco, Senegal, Ivory Coast, South Africa, and Namibia are countries rich enough to be able to export their fish. The Great Lakes region has many amazing freshwater fish, too. Countries such as Tanzania, Uganda, Kenya, and Nigeria catch these freshwater fish.

Timber Production

In recent years, African forests have been in danger from people who have begun to cut down a large number of trees. Areas of forest that are near sea ports or larger local markets have lost the greatest numbers of trees.

In the Central African Republic, for example, between 15 and 18 different types of tree are being cut down, while in the Democratic Republic of Congo, 18 to 20 species are disappearing. Many environmental groups fear that these actions will destroy the habitats of many species of animal, especially the gorilla, whose numbers are dwindling.

Peasant Women

Around 70 percent of farm work in the region is done by women. However, most of the income from agriculture is controlled by men. This tradition has led to great inequalities between men and women in their households.

A lumberjack cutting a tree with a chainsaw.

CAIRO

Located on the Nile River, Cairo is the largest city in the Arab world and Africa. Rich in ancient monuments, theaters, and museums, this historic center was declared a World Heritage Site by UNESCO.

Country	Egypt
Area	175 sq mi
Population	7,010,000
Density	40,080 people/sq mi

CITY EMBLEMS

The Alabaster Mosque

Built between 1830 and 1848, this mosque consists of a central dome surrounded by four others, and has two equal minarets that stand 269 feet tall. Below, you can see the front and inside of the building.

The Cairo Tower
Located in the Zamalek district, this television tower is 617 feet tall. On the fourteenth floor there is a revolving restaurant.

Mosque of Al-Azhar

This mosque was built almost 1040 years ago. Its name means "the most splendid."

Mosque of Al-Azhar
The mosque is in the center of the city.

Madrasa al-Taybarsiyya

Originally designed to complement the mosque of Al-Azhar, the Madrasa al-Taybarsiyya was built in 1309. It houses the tomb of Prince Amir Taybars.

Street Fairs

The souk, or market, of Cairo is a maze of narrow streets and tiny shops filled with goods of all kinds, such as slippers, scarves, glass pipes, spices, or jewelry.

The Egyptian Museum

This museum holds the greatest collection of objects from ancient Egypt, and has more than 120,000 pieces. Over 2.5 million people visit the museum every year.

Minaret Qaitbay

Built in 1483, this cylindrical tower has three balconies and arched panels. It was from these towers that the call to prayer came.

Egyptian Pastries

Egyptian bakeries are famous for their delicate pastries, which are made of almonds, honey, cereals, and grits.

A THOUSAND MINARETS
Cairo is known as the city of "the thousand minarets," which refers to the number of mosques in the city.

Religion

The majority of the city's population are Muslim. These girls are wearing traditional Muslim veils.

Demography

The inhabitants are mostly descendants of the ancient Egyptians, Arabs, Bedouins, and Berbers.

THE PYRAMIDS OF GIZA

Opposite the city of Cairo, across the Nile River, the mighty pyramids of Giza rise majestically. Built 4500 years ago, the pyramids house the tombs of the **pharaohs** Khufu, Khafre, and Menkaure. They are the greatest symbol of the culture of ancient Egypt.

MAP OF THE VALLEY OF THE KINGS

Location

The valley is home to the three most famous Egyptian pyramids: Khufu, Khufu's son, Khafre, and Menkaure. The map below shows how the complex was laid out.

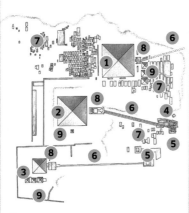

1. Pyramid of Khufu
2. Pyramid of Khafre
3. Pyramid of Menkaure
4. Great Sphinx
5. Great Temple
6. Procession route
7. Tomb of a dignitary
8. Mortuary temple
9. Secondary pyramid

The Great Sphinx
Carved from a single rock, it has the body of a lion and a human face

3,297,343 cubic yds

The total volume of the pyramid of Khufu.

Gold peak

The white limestone at the top was covered with a shiny metal, possibly gold.

Khufu

Two million stones, each weighing 440 pounds, were used to build this pyramid. The pyramid is the same height as a 40-story building.

Small pyramids

East of the pyramid of Khufu, three other smaller pyramids were found.

TECHNICAL CONSTRUCTION

Ramp System
No one is sure quite how the pyramids were built, but it is known that large blocks of stone were loaded using a complex system of ramps.

Possible ramp methods

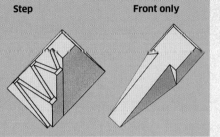

Multiple	Perimeter	Step	Front only

Khafre
The pyramid of Khafre is guarded by the Great Sphinx, a symbol of the pharaoh.

Destination
The pyramids were built to protect the dead pharoah's body. Khufu's pyramid took 33 years to build.

Menkaure
In Menkaure's burial chamber, an empty sarcophagus (stone coffin) was found.

VILLAGE
Near the Sphinx, there was a town where officials and the workers responsible for the construction of the pyramids lived.

Spectacular sight
The pyramids at sunset.

OCEANIA INTRODUCTION

Oceania is the world's smallest continent and includes Australia, New Zealand, Papua New Guinea, and many Pacific islands, including Micronesia, Fiji, Tonga, and Samoa. Before European explorers visited Oceania, the region was occupied by native people, such as the Maori. English, French, Dutch, and Portuguese people settled there, creating colonies. Many of these colonies are now independent, with their own lifestyles and cultures.

CAMPBELL ISLAND, NEW ZEALAND
THE ISLAND REMAINS UNINHABITED. THE FEW PEOPLE TO REACH ITS SHORES ARE USUALLY SCIENTISTS WHO STUDY WILDLIFE FOUND THERE.

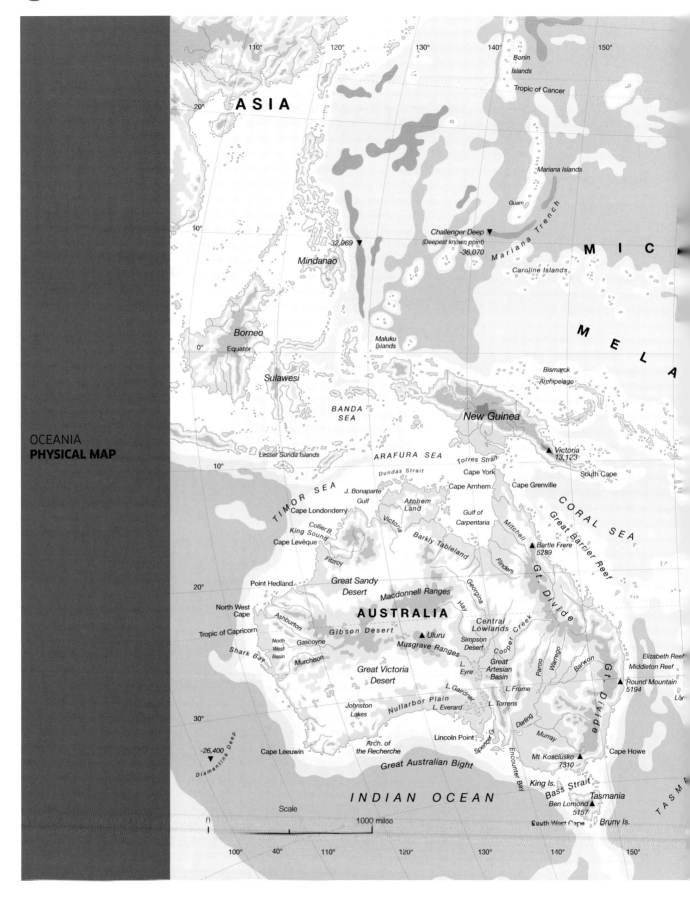

OCEANIA
PHYSICAL MAP

ASIA

110°   120°   130°   140°   150°

Bonin
Islands

20°

Tropic of Cancer

Mariana Islands

10°

Guam

Challenger Deep ▼
(Deepest known point)
-36,070

Mariana Trench

M I C

-32,969 ▼

Mindanao

Caroline Islands

M E L

Borneo

Maluku
Islands

A

0°   Equator

Bismarck
Archipelago

Sulawesi

New Guinea

BANDA
SEA

▲ Victoria
13,123

Lesser Sunda Islands

ARAFURA SEA

Torres Strait

South Cape

10°

Dundas Strait

Cape York

TIMOR SEA

J. Bonaparte
Gulf

Arnhem
Land

Cape Arnhem

Cape Grenville

CORAL SEA

Cape Londonderry

Victoria

Gulf of
Carpentaria

Mitchell

Great Barrier Reef

Collier B
King Sound

Barkly Tableland

Cape Levêque

Fitzroy

Flinders

Gt. Divide

▲ Bartle Frere
5289

20°

Point Hedland

Great Sandy
Desert

Macdonnell Ranges

Georgina

North West
Cape

AUSTRALIA

Hay

Central
Lowlands

Ashburton

Cooper Creek

Tropic of Capricorn

Gibson Desert

▲ Uluru

Simpson
Desert

Elizabeth Reef
Middleton Reef

North
West
Basin

Gascoyne

Musgrave Ranges

Great
Artesian
Basin

Paroo

Warrego

Barwon

▲ Round Mountain
5194

Shark Bay

Murchison

L.
Eyre

Gt. Divide

Lör

Great Victoria
Desert

L. Gairdner

L. Frome

Darling

30°

Johnston
Lakes

Nullarbor Plain

L. Everard

L. Torrens

Murray

Cape Howe

-26,400 ▼

Lincoln Point

Spencer G.

Mt Kosciusko ▲
7310

Cape Leeuwin

Arch. of
the Recherche

Encounter Bay

King Is.

Bass Strait

TASMA

Diamantina Deep

Great Australian Bight

Tasmania

INDIAN OCEAN

Ben Lomond ▲
5157

Bruny Is.

Scale

South West Cape

1000 miles

100°   40°   110°   120°   130°   140°   150°

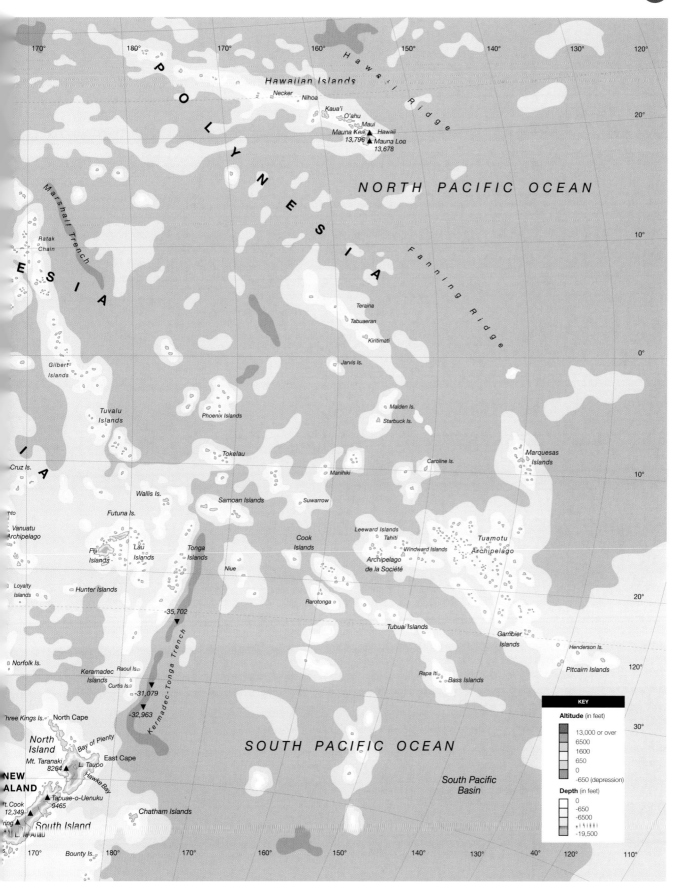

P O L Y N E S I A

Marshall Trench

Hawaiian Islands

Necker   Nihoa

Kaua'i
O'ahu   Maui
Mauna Kea ▲   Hawaii
13,796   ▲ Mauna Loa
                13,678

NORTH PACIFIC OCEAN

Fanning Ridge

Hawaii Ridge

Ratak
Chain

E
S
I
A

Gilbert
Islands

Teraina

Tabuaeran

Kiritimati

Jarvis Is.

Tuvalu
Islands

Phoenix Islands

Malden Is.

Starbuck Is.

Marquesas
Islands

Cruz Is.

I
A

Tokelau

Manihiki

Caroline Is.

Wallis Is.

Samoan Islands

Suwarrow

Futuna Is.

Leeward Islands
Tahiti

Tuamotu
Archipelago

Vanuatu
Archipelago

Fiji
Islands

Lau
Islands

Tonga
Islands

Cook
Islands

Windward Islands

Archipelago
de la Société

nto

Niue

Loyalty
Islands

Hunter Islands

Rarotonga

Tubuai Islands

Gambier
Islands

Henderson Is.

Norfolk Is.

-35,702

Keramadec
Islands   Raoul Is.

Curtis Is.

-31,079

-32,963

Kermadec-Tonga Trench

Rapa Iti   Bass Islands

Pitcairn Islands

Three Kings Is.   North Cape

North
Island

Bay of Plenty

Mt. Taranaki
8264 ▲   East Cape

L. Taupo

Hawke Bay

SOUTH PACIFIC OCEAN

South Pacific
Basin

NEW
ALAND

t. Cook
12,349 ▲

ring ▲

Tapuae-o-Uenuku
9465

Chatham Islands

South Island

L. Te Anau

Bounty Is.

KEY		

Altitude (in feet)

13,000 or over
6500
1600
650
0
-650 (depression)

Depth (in feet)

0
-650
-6500
-19,500

170°   180°   170°   160°   150°   140°   130°   120°
20°
10°
0°
10°
20°
30°
120°

170°   180°   170°   160°   150°   140°   130°   40°   120°   110°

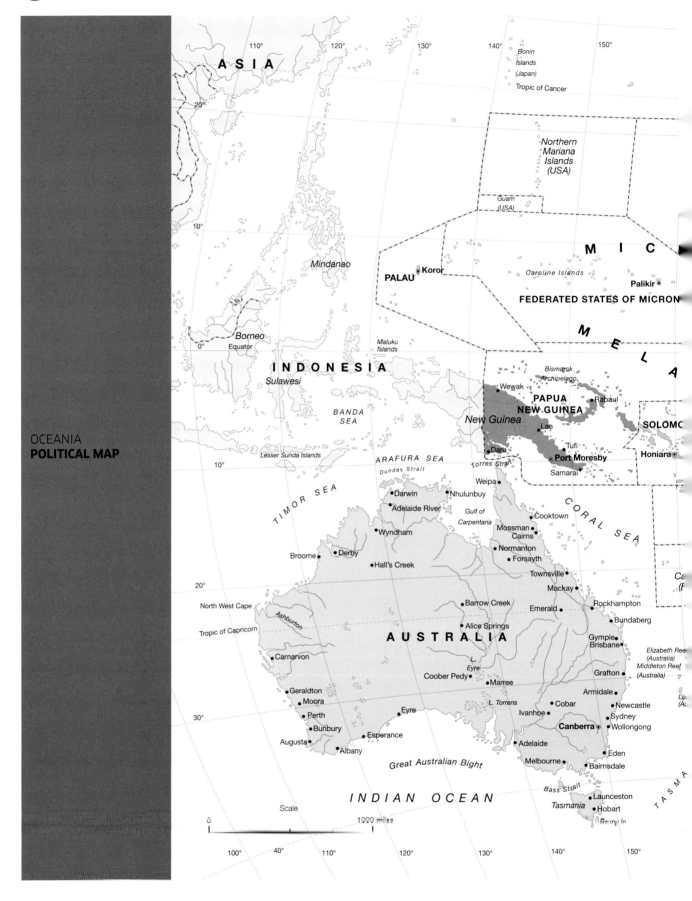

OCEANIA
POLITICAL MAP

ASIA

110°   120°   130°   140°   150°

Bonin
Islands
(Japan)

Tropic of Cancer

20°

Northern
Mariana
Islands
(USA)

10°

Guam
(USA)

M I C

Mindanao

Caroline Islands

PALAU • Koror

Palikir ⊙

FEDERATED STATES OF MICRON

Borneo
0°   Equator

M E L A

INDONESIA

Bismarck
Archipelago

Sulawesi

Maluku
Islands

Wewak

PAPUA
NEW GUINEA

• Rabaul

BANDA
SEA

New Guinea

SOLOMO

• Lae

Lesser Sunda Islands

10°

ARAFURA SEA

Torres Strait

• Daru

⊙ Port Moresby

Honiara ⊙

Dundas Strait

Samarai

Weipa •

Timor Sea

• Darwin   • Nhulunbuy

• Adelaide River

Gulf of
Carpentaria

Cooktown •

CORAL SEA

Mossman •
Cairns •

• Wyndham

Broome •   • Derby

Normanton •

Ca
(P

• Hall's Creek

• Forsayth

Townsville •

20°

Mackay •

North West Cape

Ashburton

Barrow Creek •

Emerald •

Rockhampton •

Tropic of Capricorn

• Alice Springs

Bundaberg •

AUSTRALIA

Gympie •
Brisbane •

Elizabeth Ree
(Australia)
Middleton Reef
(Australia)

• Carnarvon

L.
Eyre

Coober Pedy •

Grafton •

Lo
(Au

• Geraldton
• Moora

• Marree

Armidale •

Eyre •

L. Torrens

• Cobar

• Newcastle

30°

• Perth
• Bunbury

Ivanhoe •

Sydney •

Augusta •

• Esperance

Canberra ⊙ • Wollongong

Albany •

• Adelaide

Great Australian Bight

Melbourne •

• Eden

• Bairnsdale

INDIAN OCEAN

Bass Strait

Launceston •

Tasmania   • Hobart

T A S M A

Bruny Is

Scale

0   1000 miles

100°   40°   110°   120°   130°   140°   150°

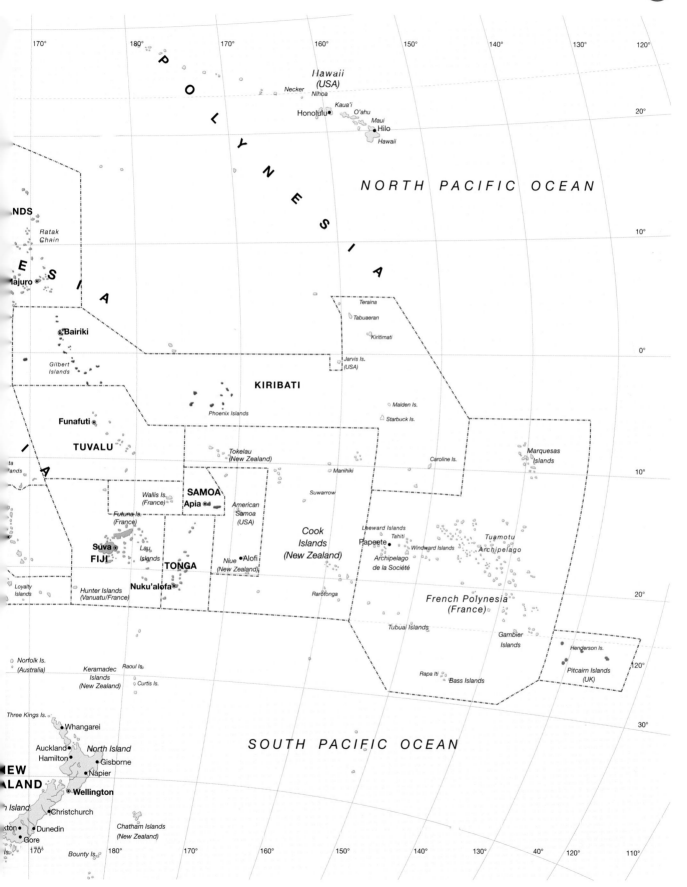

170° 180° 170° 160° 150° 140° 130° 120°

P O L Y N E S I A

Hawaii
(USA)

Necker
Nihoa

Kaua'i
Honolulu● *O'ahu*
Maui
●Hilo
Hawaii

20°

N O R T H   P A C I F I C   O C E A N

10°

NDS

Ratak
Chain

E
S
Majuro◉

Teraina

A

Tabuaeran

●Bairiki

Kiritimati

0°

Gilbert
Islands

Jarvis Is.
(USA)

KIRIBATI

○ *Malden Is.*

Phoenix Islands

○ *Starbuck Is.*

Funafuti◉

Marquesas
Islands

TUVALU

ta
lands

Tokelau
(New Zealand)

Caroline Is.

10°

I

A

Manihiki

Wallis Is.
(France)

SAMOA
Apia◉

American
Samoa
(USA)

Suwarrow

Futuna Is.
(France)

Leeward Islands
Tahiti

Tuamotu
Archipelago

Suva◉
FIJI

Lau
Islands

TONGA

Niue ●Alofi
(New Zealand)

Cook
Islands
(New Zealand)

Papeete●
Windward Islands

Archipelago
de la Société

Loyalty
Islands

Nuku'alofa◉

Hunter Islands
(Vanuatu/France)

Rarotonga

French Polynesia
(France)

20°

Tubuai Islands

Gambier
Islands

120°

○ *Norfolk Is.*
(Australia)

Keramadec
Islands
(New Zealand)

Raoul Is.

Curtis Is.

Rapa Iti
●*Bass Islands*

Henderson Is.
●●
●●
Pitcairn Islands
(UK)

Three Kings Is.

●Whangarei

30°

NEW

Auckland● *North Island*
Hamilton● ●Gisborne

S O U T H   P A C I F I C   O C E A N

LAND

●Napier

◉**Wellington**

h Island

●Christchurch

kton
●Dunedin
●Gore
Is. 170° *Bounty Is.* 180° 170° 160° 150° 140° 130° 40° 120° 110°

Chatham Islands
(New Zealand)

GEOLOGY AND LANDSCAPE

Originally, Oceania and Antarctica were one landmass called Gondwana. As a result of continental drift, lands split apart into the many volcanic islands and coral reefs that are found in the Pacific Ocean today.

Blue Mountains Australia's Blue Mountains have been declared a Natural Heritage Site by UNESCO.

MOUNTAINS AND SNOW
AUSTRALIA

Three Sisters

These rock formations are found in the Blue Mountains in the Australian state of New South Wales. Each "sister" is just over 2953 feet high. They were formed when the sandstone eroded.

NATIONAL PARKS
NEW ZEALAND

Tongariro and Its Holy Sites

Tongariro on the North Island is New Zealand's oldest national park. It holds a great spiritual importance for the original inhabitants of New Zealand, the Maori. The park has three active volcanoes, which add to its natural beauty. Visitors to the park can walk along the many trails, and for the more adventurous, there is whitewater rafting.

NATURAL RESOURCES
TOURISM IN PROTECTED AREAS

Arthur's Pass, New Zealand

Arthur's Pass is the highest pass over New Zealand's Southern Alps. It is named after Arthur Dudley Dobson, who found his way over the pass in 1864, but the route was already known to the Maori. The highest peak in the Southern Alps is the 7874-foot-high Mount Murchison. Popular activities include rock climbing, mountain biking, and hiking.

GEOGRAPHY AND CLIMATE
THE WORLD'S SMALLEST CONTINENT

Great Eastern Ranges, Australia

The Great Dividing Range (above) is the third-longest mountain range in the world. It stretches almost the entire length of Australia's east coast. The highest peak in the country, the 7310-foot-high Mount Kosciuszko (left) is found here.

Great Barrier Reef
Off the coast of northeastern Australia, the Great Barrier Reef is the largest living coral reef in the world.

SEAS AND VOLCANOES
POLLUTION WATCH

Timor Sea

Located between the island of Timor and Australia, the Timor Sea borders the Indian Ocean. In 2009, there was a major oil spill there, which had a disastrous effect on birds, marine invertebrates, coral, and algae.

Mount Egmont, New Zealand

Called Taranaki by the Maori, Mount Egmont is a dormant volcano, 8261 feet high. The volcano was last active in 1655. Other active volcanoes on the North Island include Ruapehu, Ngauruhoe, and Tongariro.

Uluru
Found in central Australia, this red sandstone rock is sacred to the Aboriginal people of the area.

AUSTRALIA
ULURU

Sacred Rock

Located in Australia's Northern Territory, Uluru is just one of the attractions of the Uluru-Kata Tjuta National Park. This giant red rock stands 1142 feet high. Considered one of the most important sites in Aboriginal culture, the rock is frequently visited by Aboriginals for ceremonies and rituals.

FLORA AND FAUNA

Some exotic plants and animals came to Oceania with the arrival of foreign explorers and settlers. However, Australia still has many species that are found nowhere else, including the kangaroo, the Tasmanian devil, and the koala bear.

Lupins
These striking plants were brought to New Zealand by settlers from Europe.

PROTECTED SPECIES
LIVING FOSSILS

Reptile

The tuatara lizard is found in New Zealand. Its name means "spiny back" in Maori. It grows to 27.5 inches long and is considered a living fossil because it is not found anywhere else on the planet.

EXOTIC SPECIES
NOW A PEST

Mynah Bird

The mynah bird is native to Asia. It was introduced to the region by the British to control crop pests. Today, this bird is considered to be a pest in both rural and urban areas and is a threat to the native bird species of Oceania.

MOVIE MAGIC
FINDING NEMO

Clownfish

The clownfish lives in the Pacific Ocean. Easily recognized by their bright orange color, clownfish are carnivorous and live with sea anemones on the coral reefs of the Pacific.

Frigate Bird

The frigate bird is a symbol on the flag of the island nation of Kiribati. It is easily identified by its swollen red throat.

BIRD OF PARADISE
The bird of paradise is the national bird of Papua New Guinea.

Brown Booby

The brown booby bird is found along the coastlines of Tuvalu, Micronesia, French Polynesia, and Australia. Brown boobies eat mainly small fish or squid that gather in groups near the surface of the ocean.

Surgeonfish

Diversity

There are 1500 species of fish and 2200 plant species living on the Great Barrier Reef.

Angelfish

Butterflyfish

Tasmanian Devil

The Tasmanian devil is an aggressive carnivorous **marsupial**. It is found only on the island of Tasmania, off the coast of southern Australia.

Koala

This plant-eating marsupial grows up to 29.5 inches long.

Saltwater crocodile
The saltwater crocodile is the largest and most dangerous crocodile in the world.

Kiwi

The kiwi bird is the official symbol of New Zealand. The kiwi is a very rare bird that is active mainly at night. Kiwi birds cannot fly because their wings are too small.

Eucalyptus
The eucalyptus is the most common native tree in Australia.

POPULATION AND ECONOMY

Australia and New Zealand are the largest countries in Oceania, but they have some of the lowest population densities. These two countries have developed and stable economies with strong trade links to Southeast Asia. Many of the smaller countries and colonies in Oceania struggle to get by on income from tourism and agriculture.

Sydney, Australia
Pedestrians cross between George Street and Park Avenue, in the heart of the city.

NEW ZEALAND
CITIES

Auckland

The largest city in New Zealand, Auckland has two ports. It is also the economic and cultural center of the country.

Government

In 1893, New Zealand became the first country in the world to recognize the right of women to vote. While some colonies are fighting for independence, most countries in the region are democracies.

Boat Taxis

These are used by the people of Micronesia to get around. They are also rented out to tourists visiting the islands.

Australian Industry

Australia is the most advanced country in the region. It has large chemical, petrochemical, food, and beverage industries.

New Zealand
This country is one of the largest sheep farming nations in the world.

CONTRASTING INFRASTRUCTURE

Houghton Highway

The longest bridge in Oceania is the Houghton Highway in Queensland, Australia. This **viaduct** is 8990 feet long. While Australia has 505,157 miles of road, Tuvalu has just 5 miles. Most countries in the region trade by sea.

Wine industry
Australia is a large producer of wine. It is the fourth-largest exporter of wine in the world.

City link
The Sydney monorail runs through the city.

RICHNESS OF PEOPLE AND LANGUAGES

Micronesia

This is a group of thousands of small islands in the western Pacific Ocean. Many of the islands are now small independent nations. Micronesia has a wide variety of cultures, and its people speak many different languages. The people are descended from settlers who came from other parts of the Pacific.

MINING
A GREAT RESOURCE

Australia's Mining Industry

Australia is the second-largest gold producer in the world and the leading producer of **bauxite**, **titanium**, and diamonds. The country also mines **uranium**, nickel, lead, zinc, tin, and copper, and has its own oil fields. These natural resources are very important to the country's economy.

ABORIGINAL AUSTRALIANS

Aboriginal Australians were the first people to settle in Australia. Traditionally, they lived as hunter-gatherers, hunting and foraging food from the land. There are many different Aboriginal groups across the continent, each with its own language and traditions.

COMMON HERITAGE

Out of Africa

About 80,000 years ago, a small group of people left Africa and crossed into Arabia in search of food. All non-Africans, from Europeans to Amerindians to Aboriginal Australians, are descended from this group. Some of the people who left Africa at this time moved along the southern coast of Asia, reaching Australia about 50,000 years ago. These were the ancestors of today's Aboriginal Australian people.

CULTURE AND TRADITIONS

Body Painting

Body decoration using ancestral designs is an important part of many ceremonies. Designs are painted onto the face and body using ochers (natural clays) that are ground and mixed with water.

Aboriginal culture
Boys perform a traditional dance.

Dance

Dance is an important part of Aboriginal culture. Dancing may be part of a social gathering or to mark a specific occasion, such as the opening of a new building.

Cave Art

These rock paintings in Kakadu National Park represent scenes from a mythical world. The paintings are many thousands of years old.

Didgeridoo

This wind instrument is used in dance and music. A didgeridoo may be 2.5–6.5 feet long. The larger the instrument, the deeper its sound.

Stone Mortar

A stone mortar was traditionally used to grind or crush herbs and seeds used for cooking.

Men and women

Male dancing is lively with a lot of jumping and kicking. Women have their own dances, which are less energetic and more of a loose-knee shuffle.

Homes

In the past, Aboriginal people did not build houses or huts but lived in caves. Today, many Aborigines still live in the Australian **outback**, but in houses.

Boomerang

This flat, wooden weapon was traditionally used for hunting. The boomerang was thrown at its target. If it missed, the boomerang would spin around and return to the person who had thrown it.

THE SYDNEY OPERA HOUSE

One of the world's most recognizable buildings, the Sydney Opera House contains a large hall for opera, a concert hall, large and small theaters, an exhibition area, and a library.

BUILDING DETAILS

A Palace of Culture
The Sydney Opera House was declared a World Heritage Site by UNESCO in 2007.

Fact File
Location:
Sydney, Australia

Kind of building:
Cultural center

Capacity (of performing spaces):
5700 spectators

Structure:
Cement, pink granite, and wood veneer

City postcard
The Sydney Opera House was opened in 1973. It cost AU$102 million to build.

Utzon Hall (opera house)
In 2004, the old hall was renamed after the Opera House's architect. The Utzon Hall is used to host a range of events, including musical performances.

❶ Opera house
❷ Concert hall
❸ Restaurant

Uses
The Opera House hosts opera, ballet, concerts, and theater in five halls. There are also rooms for conferences and meetings.

Construction
The Sydney Opera House was built in stages between 1959 and 1973. The original architect was Jorn Utzon, from Denmark.

233
The number of architects who submitted designs for the Opera House.

Auditorium (concert hall)

New Colonnade
The new western colonnade opened in 2006. The new walkway is 148 feet long. It runs along the side of the building, allowing light to flood in and giving people visiting the Opera House views of Sydney Harbour.

The Concert Hall
This magnificent venue can hold 2679 concert-goers. It is the Opera House's largest interior venue, and is home to the Sydney Symphony Orchestra and the Australian Chamber Orchestra.

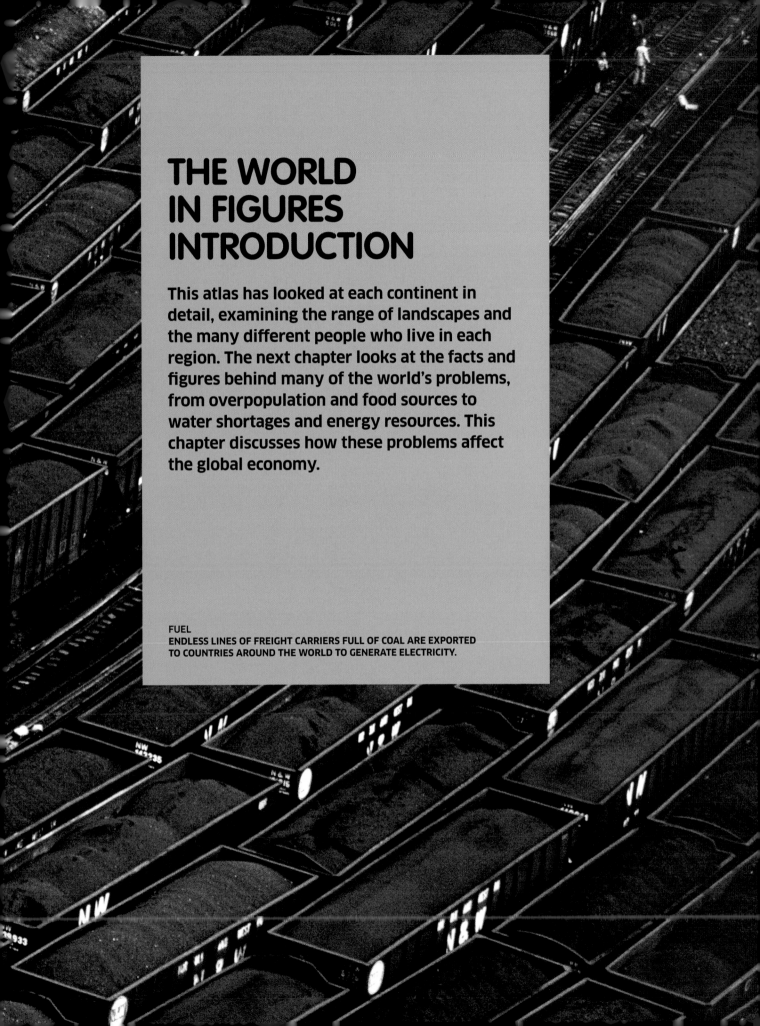

THE WORLD
IN FIGURES
INTRODUCTION

This atlas has looked at each continent in detail, examining the range of landscapes and the many different people who live in each region. The next chapter looks at the facts and figures behind many of the world's problems, from overpopulation and food sources to water shortages and energy resources. This chapter discusses how these problems affect the global economy.

FUEL
ENDLESS LINES OF FREIGHT CARRIERS FULL OF COAL ARE EXPORTED
TO COUNTRIES AROUND THE WORLD TO GENERATE ELECTRICITY.

CONTINENTS AND COUNTRIES

Humankind has made all kinds of divisions and boundaries that shape the world map politically. While many of the borders have names that have existed naturally, some have been formed as a result of historical events, such as war.

BORDERS
Usually shown as lines on a map, borders mark the geographic areas that define separate countries.

The Land Area

Most of the Earth's surface is covered in water. The land area, representing about one-third of the Earth, is divided into seven continents. Central America and the Caribbean is sometimes considered a subcontinent and is part of the continent of North America.

38
million

The number of times that the world's largest country, Russia, is greater than the Vatican City, the world's smallest country.

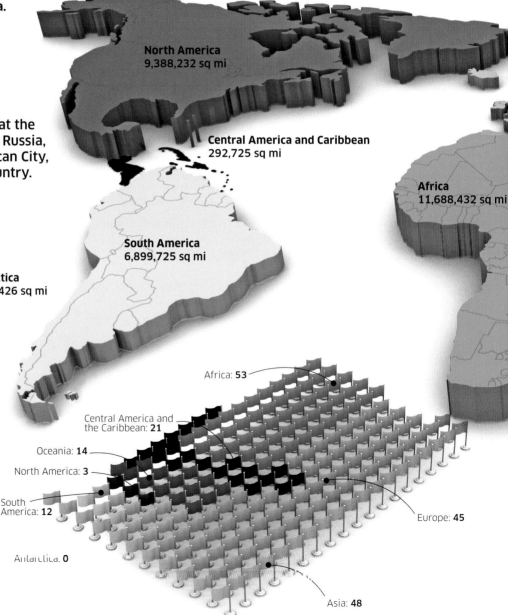

North America
9,388,232 sq mi

Central America and Caribbean
292,725 sq mi

Africa
11,688,432 sq mi

South America
6,899,725 sq mi

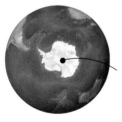

Antarctica
5,495,426 sq mi

Africa: **53**

Central America and the Caribbean: **21**

Oceania: **14**

North America: **3**

South America: **12**

Antarctica: **0**

Europe: **45**

Asia: **48**

MANY COUNTRIES

Each flag in the illustration on the right represents a country, colored to match the continent or subcontinent it belongs to. Antarctica is unique in having no individual countries.

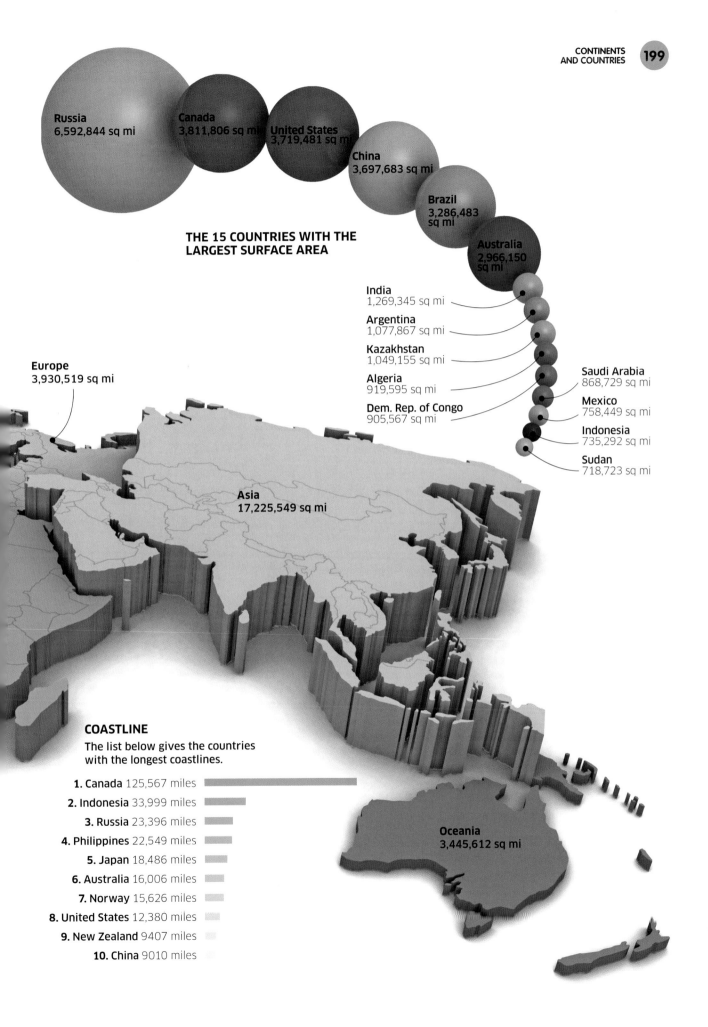

Russia
6,592,844 sq mi

Canada
3,811,806 sq mi

United States
3,719,481 sq mi

China
3,697,683 sq mi

Brazil
3,286,483 sq mi

Australia
2,966,150 sq mi

THE 15 COUNTRIES WITH THE LARGEST SURFACE AREA

India
1,269,345 sq mi

Argentina
1,077,867 sq mi

Kazakhstan
1,049,155 sq mi

Algeria
919,595 sq mi

Dem. Rep. of Congo
905,567 sq mi

Saudi Arabia
868,729 sq mi

Mexico
758,449 sq mi

Indonesia
735,292 sq mi

Sudan
718,723 sq mi

Europe
3,930,519 sq mi

Asia
17,225,549 sq mi

Oceania
3,445,612 sq mi

COASTLINE

The list below gives the countries with the longest coastlines.

1. Canada 125,567 miles
2. Indonesia 33,999 miles
3. Russia 23,396 miles
4. Philippines 22,549 miles
5. Japan 18,486 miles
6. Australia 16,006 miles
7. Norway 15,626 miles
8. United States 12,380 miles
9. New Zealand 9407 miles
10. China 9010 miles

CLIMATE ZONES

Different parts of the world can be divided into climate zones. These are regions where there is a similar temperature, atmospheric pressure, rainfall, and other precipitation and humidity.

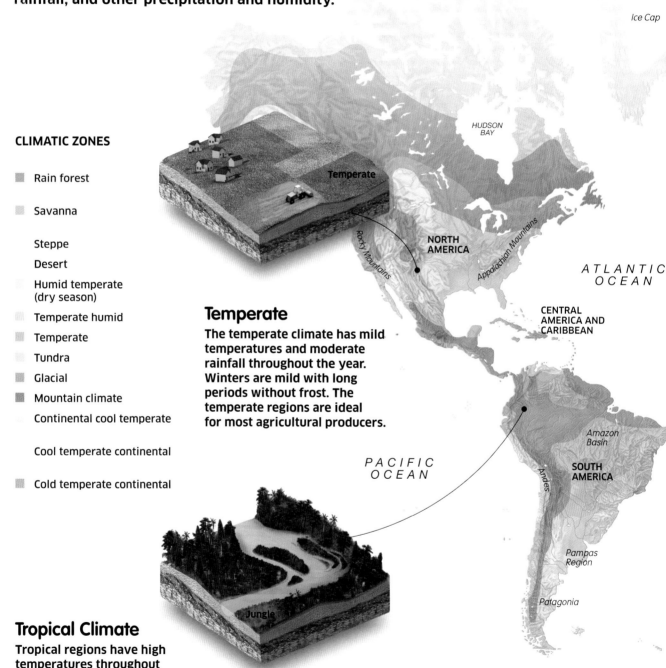

Ice Cap

CLIMATIC ZONES

- Rain forest
- Savanna
- Steppe
- Desert
- Humid temperate (dry season)
- Temperate humid
- Temperate
- Tundra
- Glacial
- Mountain climate
- Continental cool temperate
- Cool temperate continental
- Cold temperate continental

HUDSON BAY

Temperate

Rocky Mountains

NORTH AMERICA

Appalachian Mountains

ATLANTIC OCEAN

CENTRAL AMERICA AND CARIBBEAN

Amazon Basin

PACIFIC OCEAN

Andes

SOUTH AMERICA

Pampas Region

Patagonia

Jungle

Temperate

The temperate climate has mild temperatures and moderate rainfall throughout the year. Winters are mild with long periods without frost. The temperate regions are ideal for most agricultural producers.

Tropical Climate

Tropical regions have high temperatures throughout the year, combined with heavy rains. About half of the world's population lives in tropical climates. Here, the vegetation is lush and there is a very high level of moisture caused by rainfall and plant transpiration.

Extreme Temperatures

The highest temperature was recorded in Libya in 1922: 136 °F. The lowest temperature was recorded in 1983 at Vostok Station, Antarctica (-128.6 °F). The area of Marble Bar in Western Australia has a constant high temperature. From October 7, 1923 to April 31, 1924, the temperature was never lower than 100 °F.

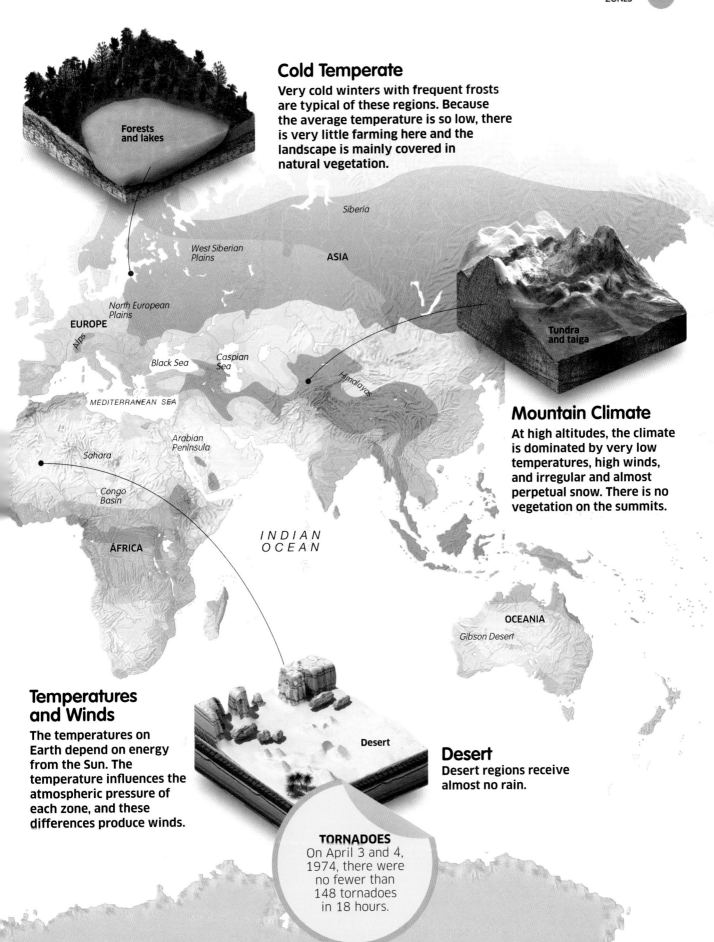

Cold Temperate

Very cold winters with frequent frosts are typical of these regions. Because the average temperature is so low, there is very little farming here and the landscape is mainly covered in natural vegetation.

Forests and lakes

Siberia

West Siberian Plains

ASIA

North European Plains

EUROPE

Alps

Black Sea

Caspian Sea

MEDITERRANEAN SEA

Himalayas

Tundra and taiga

Mountain Climate

At high altitudes, the climate is dominated by very low temperatures, high winds, and irregular and almost perpetual snow. There is no vegetation on the summits.

Sahara

Arabian Peninsula

Congo Basin

INDIAN OCEAN

ÁFRICA

OCEANIA

Gibson Desert

Temperatures and Winds

The temperatures on Earth depend on energy from the Sun. The temperature influences the atmospheric pressure of each zone, and these differences produce winds.

Desert

Desert

Desert regions receive almost no rain.

TORNADOES

On April 3 and 4, 1974, there were no fewer than 148 tornadoes in 18 hours.

OVERPOPULATION

As the world population continues to increase, the pressure to meet the basic needs of life will become greater. The differences between the standard of living of the most economically developed countries and the least developed countries will remain high, because the population will grow even more in poor countries.

Japan
Crowded streets in Tokyo.

DIFFERENT VALUES

Life Expectancy

This is the average number of years a person is expected to live. In Europe, during the time of the Roman Empire, the average life expectancy was 25 years. In 1900, it reached 50 across the world. Thanks to many advances in medicine, the average life expectancy now stands at 67 years. Nevertheless, there are big differences between the life expectancies of the rich and poor.

The Future
By 2050, the United Nations predicts that the population of the Earth will be 9.1 billion people.

Asia at the Head

East Asia has the highest concentration of people in the world.

A World of Difference

Life expectancy in some countries:

COUNTRY	AGE
JAPAN	82
SWITZERLAND	81
UNITED STATES	78
ARGENTINA	75
VENEZUELA	73
MONGOLIA	67
NIGERIA	47

Overcrowding

With nearly 17 million people in Calcutta, India, problems such as poverty, water pollution, traffic, and noise are common.

Solutions

Solutions to problems such as food, water, and energy shortages—and also poor healthcare and education—need to be found to support the ever-growing global population.

COUNTRIES WITH MOST PEOPLE

Two-thirds of the world population live in just 16 countries.

- 3.5% Indonesia
- 4.5% United States of America
- 18% India
- 19% China
- 55% Rest of the world

URBAN GEOGRAPHY

Huge City

A **conurbation** is the result of growth and expansion of a central city. Neighboring towns or cities that have developed are absorbed to form a single unit.

CONURBATIONS	PEOPLE
Tokyo, Japan	38,000,000
Guangzhou, China	24,500,000
Seoul, South Korea	24,200,000
Mexico City, Mexico	23,400,000
New Delhi, India	23,200,000

AGRICULTURE

The production of **genetically modified (GM) crops** is increasing. Scientists believe that genetic modification can improve crops, and reduce costs and the amount of chemicals used. Some environmentalists warn that not enough is known about the effect of GM crops on the environment and on consumers.

NO LIMITS
The production of GM crops has affected both industrialized and developing countries.

Countries with GM Crops

This map shows the distribution of GM crops in 2010, in millions of acres.

Canada 22

United States 165

France 0.12

Spain 0.25

Portugal 0.1

Mexico 0.25

Honduras 0.12

ATLANTIC OCEAN

Colombia 0.12

Bolivia 2.2

Brazil 63

Paraguay 6.4

Chile 0.12

Uruguay 2.7

PACIFIC OCEAN

Argentina 57

PERCENTAGE OF FARMED LAND IN ARGENTINA

54% GM crops (soy, corn, and cotton)

46% Natural crops

NATURAL AND GM SOY AND COTTON CROPS AROUND THE WORLD

Soy

24% Natural

76% GM

Cotton

62% GM

38% Natural

90

The percentage of all GM crops produced in Argentina, Brazil, the United States, and Canada.

TOP PRODUCERS OF WHEAT
In millions of tons per year

1. China 112
2. India 79
3. USA 68
4. Russia 64
5. France 39
6. Canada 29
7. Germany 26
8. Ukraine 26
9. Australia 21
10. Pakistan 21

TOP PRODUCERS OF POTATOES
In millions of tons per year

1. China 72
2. Russia 36
3. India 26
4. USA 20
5. Ukraine 19
6. Poland 11
7. Germany 11
8. Belarus 8
9. Netherlands 7
10. France 6

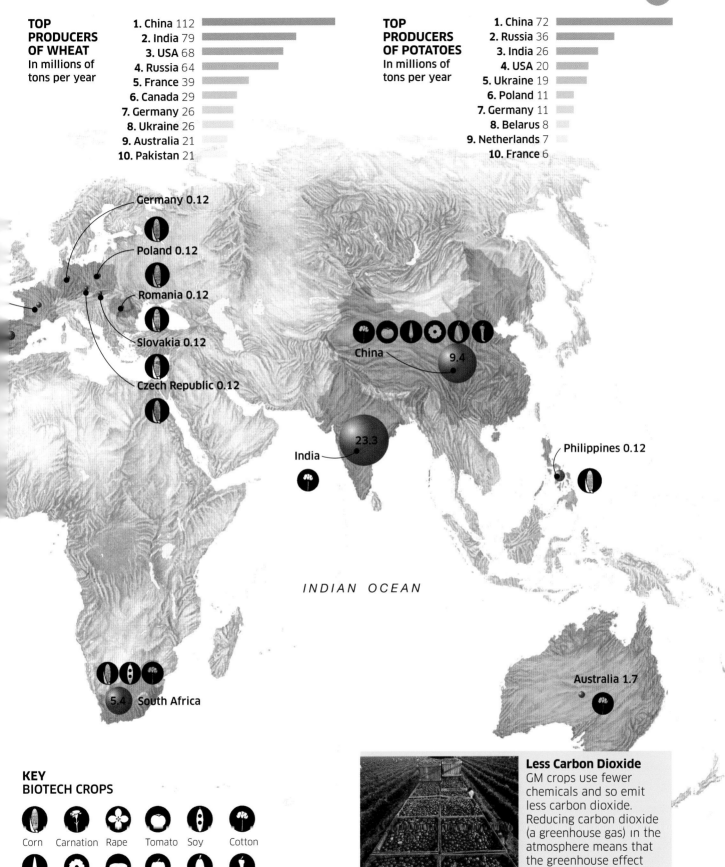

Germany 0.12
Poland 0.12
Romania 0.12
Slovakia 0.12
Czech Republic 0.12
China 9.4
India 23.3
Philippines 0.12
South Africa 5.4
Australia 1.7

INDIAN OCEAN

KEY BIOTECH CROPS

Corn | Carnation | Rape | Tomato | Soy | Cotton
Poplar | Petunia | Alfalfa | Pumpkin | Papaya | Pepper

Less Carbon Dioxide
GM crops use fewer chemicals and so emit less carbon dioxide. Reducing carbon dioxide (a greenhouse gas) in the atmosphere means that the greenhouse effect has less impact.

FISHING

In its global report on fishing, the Food and Agriculture Organization of the United Nations (FAO) stated that 19 percent of fishing resources are overexploited and 8 percent are depleted. Although the situation has remained stable since 2000, overfishing will ultimately have a serious impact on the world's food supply.

All at Sea

The seas and oceans provide 90 percent of fish that is caught. The remaining 10 percent come from freshwater sources. The environmental charity Greenpeace has called for a law to protect 40 percent of the oceans from overfishing.

Hungry Oceans

Due to the overfishing of anchovy and mackerel, natural predators of these fish are left with a decreasing source of food. This has affected both dolphins and tuna.

Shrimp Farming

The world shrimp production has stabilized as a result of shrimp farming. India, China, the United States, Thailand, Indonesia, Mexico, Malaysia, Japan, Vietnam, and Brazil are the leading countries engaged in shrimp farming.

MAJOR EXPORTERS (2008)

These are the annual figures of the top fish-exporting countries, in billions of dollars.

1. China 10.1
2. Norway 6.9
3. Thailand 6.5
4. Denmark 4.6
5. Vietnam 4.5
6. USA 4.5

Work

Fishing is very important to the livelihoods of millions of people around the world. More than 60 million people are said to work in the fishing industry, and half of this workforce are women.

SOURCE OF PROTEIN

Important Values

Fish and fish products make up 15 percent of the animal protein eaten by half of the global population. This means that on average, each person eats about 37 pounds of fish each year.

LIVESTOCK

Livestock is an important resource and a good indicator of the economy of a country. It is is used for meat and other products, such as leather and wool. In less economically developed countries, animals are also used to move agricultural equipment and as a means of transportation.

PROTECTION
HEALTH

Health Problems

According to the FAO, the risk of disease being transmitted from animals to humans has increased because more animals are being reared. Influenza A is one such disease.

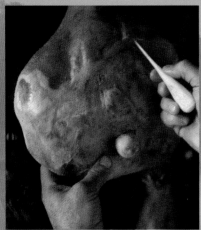

Meat Producers

There are about 1.3 billion cattle in the world. Countries such as the United States, Brazil, and China have large areas of fertile land for raising cattle.

Dairy Producers

The graph below shows the major dairy producers. Consumption of dairy products varies widely around the world. It depends on the eating habits and diet of the population as well as its wealth.

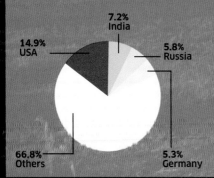

7.2%
India

14.9%
USA

5.8%
Russia

66.8%
Others

5.3%
Germany

Poultry

According to the FAO, in the last decade, the consumption of poultry products in less economically developed countries increased each year by 5.8 percent.

POULTRY PRODUCTION (in thousands of tons)

1. USA 19,691
2. China 15,052
3. Brazil 9225
4. Mexico 2585
5. India 2313

Meat Production

As the global population grows, there is an increase in the demand for meat products in less economically developed countries. The FAO reports that meat production will grow from 278 million tons a year to 463 million tons by 2050.

CHANGING STATISTICS

World Meat Consumption

The protein intake from eating meat has changed over time. In 1968, the global average of proteins from meat per person per day was 0.3 oz. In 1998, this had increased to 0.4 oz.

MEATS CONSUMED

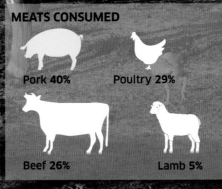

Pork 40%   Poultry 29%

Beef 26%   Lamb 5%

PER PERSON PER DAY

PLACE	OUNCES
Developed countries	7.9
Latin America	5.2
Far East and South Asia	4.0
Middle East	1.5
Developing countries	1.7
Africa	1.1

A THIRSTY WORLD

According to the World Health Organization, about 900 million people worldwide lack access to safe drinking water. Another 2.5 billion, over a third of the world's population, lack adequate sanitation systems. In some countries, water is so scarce that not a drop is wasted: the water used to wash a baby is then used for washing clothes or cleaning the kitchen.

RIGHTS
Environmental organizations believe that water is not a commodity but a basic human right.

Human Water Consumption

This map shows that the water intended for human consumption is much less than that used in agriculture and industry.

MAJOR CONSUMERS OF WATER

- Industrial use
- Industrial and agricultural use
- Industrial use, with important domestic use
- Domestic use
- Domestic and agricultural use
- Agricultural use, but with important domestic use
- Agricultural use
- Agricultural use, with important industrial use
- Agricultural use, with less important industrial use
- No data

Water Shortages
In many African countries, people have to line up each day to get water. Every year, 1.5 million children die from diarrhea and dehydration, which could have been prevented by having access to clean drinking water.

Human Health
It is estimated that to ensure a person's basic needs, such as washing, sanitation, drinking, and cooking, each person needs 5–13 gallons of clean, uncontaminated water each day.

13

The percentage of people living in Afghanistan who have access to safe drinking water.

Role of Women

Women play a key role in domestic water use, because they are often responsible for cooking, looking after children, and washing dishes, clothes, and the house. In places where there is no running water, it is often the women in the area who walk to fetch water. However, women are often left out of decisions on the planning and management of water resources.

OIL

The world's richest countries depend on oil as their main source of energy. However, we know that oil reserves are running out. As a result, the price of oil has gone up and this has affected the global economy.

Map of Oil Consumption and Production

This map shows the largest users and producers of oil. In red is the amount used each day, while blue shows the amount produced each day. The figures are the amount used or produced per day in millions of barrels (one barrel is equivalent to 42 gallons of oil).

⬤ **The biggest users**
The world uses about 85 million barrels of oil every day. The biggest user is the United States.

⬤ **The biggest producers**
Saudi Arabia, Russia, and the United States are the biggest oil producers.

▨ Main shipping routes
▨ Alternative shipping routes

70

The percentage of oil consumed in the United States that is used as fuel for transportation.

LESS OIL
Supplies of oil and natural gas (also found in oil fields) are going to become smaller over the next decade.

Canada
2264 3288

USA
20,687

8330

Mexico
1997 3707

ATLANTIC OCEAN

PACIFIC OCEAN

Venezuela
2803

Brazil
2217

USES OF OIL

Fuel
About 95 percent of the world's vehicles use fuels made from oil. As a result, the cost of transporting goods goes up when the price of oil goes up.

Making Electricity
Much of the world's electricity is made in power plants using oil or gas as fuel. These power plants need to be replaced with plants that use other sources of energy.

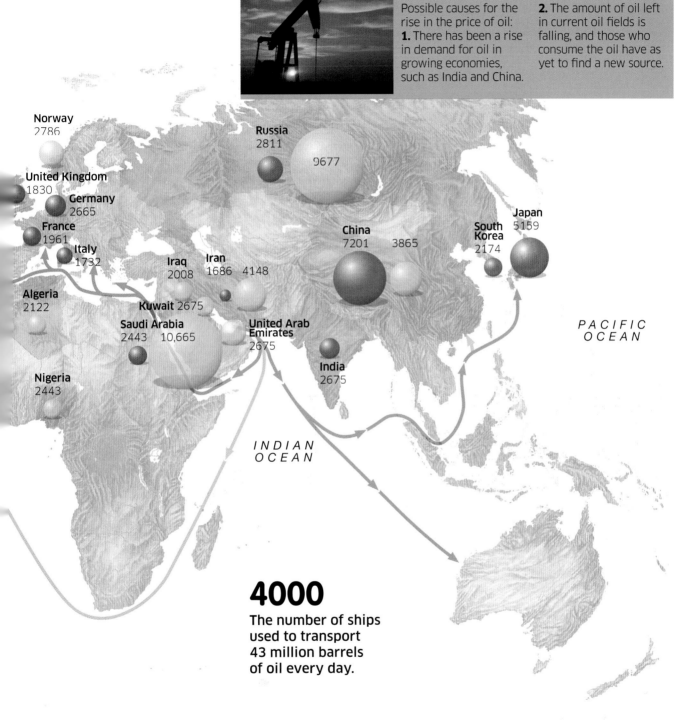

Rising Oil Prices

Possible causes for the rise in the price of oil:
1. There has been a rise in demand for oil in growing economies, such as India and China.

2. The amount of oil left in current oil fields is falling, and those who consume the oil have as yet to find a new source.

Norway 2786

Russia 2811
9677

United Kingdom 1830

Germany 2665

France 1961

Italy 1732

China 7201   3865

Japan 5159

South Korea 2174

PACIFIC OCEAN

Algeria 2122

Iraq 2008

Iran 1686   4148

Kuwait 2675

Saudi Arabia 2443   10,665

United Arab Emirates 2675

Nigeria 2443

India 2675

INDIAN OCEAN

4000
The number of ships used to transport 43 million barrels of oil every day.

Plastics

Many goods are made of plastic, which is a material made partly from oil. Scientists are now looking for other materials to use instead of plastics.

Other Uses

Oil is used to make many things, including dyes, fertilizer, and asphalt (left, used in building roads). An increase in the price of oil affects a huge number of the things that we use.

LIGHTING THE PLANET

Seen from space, the Earth is well lit by electricity. The generation of electricity by burning fossil fuels (coal, oil, and gas) has serious environmental implications. As a result, new technologies are being tested and alternative sources of energy are being sought.

NO STARS
In many cities, stars cannot be seen in the night sky due to the reflection of electric lights.

Planet of Night Light

At nightfall, in many urban settings, the sunlight is replaced by electrical lighting until the Sun rises again.

London, UK

París, France

Madrid, Spain

New York, USA

Los Angeles, USA

Miami, USA

Caracas, Venezuela

CREATING ELECTRICITY

Electricity has to be generated. To do this, different sources are used. Most of these sources, such as coal, oil, and gas, cause high levels of pollution and/or increased carbon dioxide (CO_2) emissions.

Oil (5.8%)
Accounts for 38 percent of CO_2 emissions into the atmosphere.

Other (2.3%)
These are clean and renewable energies, such as solar, wind, geothermal, and biomass.

Nuclear (14.8%)
Clean and virtually renewable but has the problem of radioactive waste and possible accidents.

Coal (41%)
The most polluting of all power sources and is responsible for 42 percent of the CO_2 emissions into the atmosphere.

Río de Janeiro, Brazil
Sao Paulo, Brazil

Buenos Aires, Argentina

Hydroelectric (16%)
It is clean and renewable but damming rivers causes ecological problems and displacement of humans.

Gas (20.1%)
It accounts for 19 percent of CO_2 emissions into the atmosphere.

65

The percentage of humans who live under electrically lit skies.

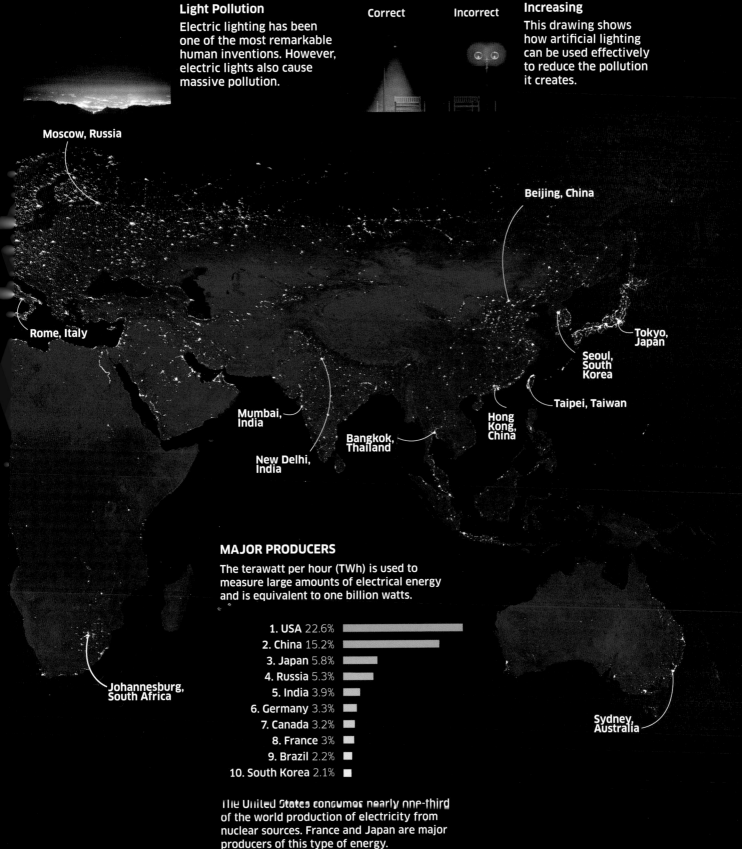

Light Pollution

Electric lighting has been one of the most remarkable human inventions. However, electric lights also cause massive pollution.

Correct   Incorrect

Increasing

This drawing shows how artificial lighting can be used effectively to reduce the pollution it creates.

Moscow, Russia

Beijing, China

Rome, Italy

Tokyo, Japan

Seoul, South Korea

Taipei, Taiwan

Mumbai, India

Hong Kong, China

Bangkok, Thailand

New Delhi, India

Johannesburg, South Africa

Sydney, Australia

MAJOR PRODUCERS

The terawatt per hour (TWh) is used to measure large amounts of electrical energy and is equivalent to one billion watts.

1. USA 22.6%
2. China 15.2%
3. Japan 5.8%
4. Russia 5.3%
5. India 3.9%
6. Germany 3.3%
7. Canada 3.2%
8. France 3%
9. Brazil 2.2%
10. South Korea 2.1%

The United States consumes nearly one-third of the world production of electricity from nuclear sources. France and Japan are major producers of this type of energy.

MAKING CONNECTIONS

According to recent research, one in four people on Earth use the Internet. This new reality has accelerated to unprecedented levels the process of globalization that is facing our world.

FACEBOOK
In 2010, according to IWS (see below), the total number of Facebook users was estimated to be 517,760,460.

Radiography of the Network

On average, 40 percent of the world's population has Internet access. However, this is not uniform and the most populous countries, with a certain level of development, have the highest access.

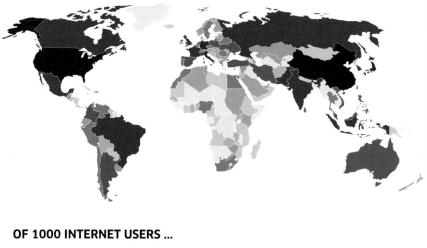

INTERNET USERS, IN MILLIONS

- Over 100
- 50 to 100
- 20 to 50
- 10 to 20
- 5 to 10
- 2–5
- 1–2
- 0.5 to 1
- 0.1 to 0.5
- 0.01 to 0.1
- Less than 0.01

OF 1000 INTERNET USERS ...

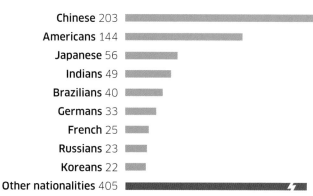

Chinese	203
Americans	144
Japanese	56
Indians	49
Brazilians	40
Germans	33
French	25
Russians	23
Koreans	22
Other nationalities	405

2011

According to Internet World Stats (IWS), there were over 3 billion Internet users.

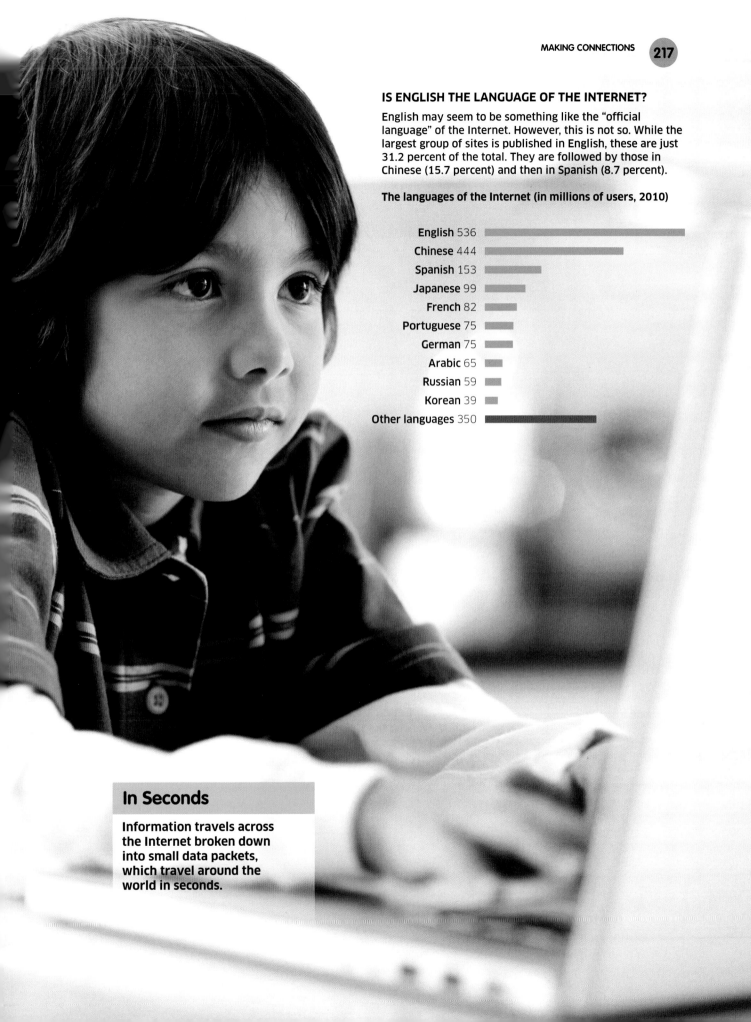

IS ENGLISH THE LANGUAGE OF THE INTERNET?

English may seem to be something like the "official language" of the Internet. However, this is not so. While the largest group of sites is published in English, these are just 31.2 percent of the total. They are followed by those in Chinese (15.7 percent) and then in Spanish (8.7 percent).

The languages of the Internet (in millions of users, 2010)

English 536
Chinese 444
Spanish 153
Japanese 99
French 82
Portuguese 75
German 75
Arabic 65
Russian 59
Korean 39
Other languages 350

In Seconds

Information travels across the Internet broken down into small data packets, which travel around the world in seconds.

GLOSSARY

ACOUSTICS
The properties or qualities of a room or building that determine how sound is transmitted in it.

ADAPTATIONS
Changes to animals and plants over a long period of time to ensure their survival in a specific biome. For example, animals found at the Poles usually have very thick coats.

AMPHITHEATER
An open, circular, or oval building, with levels of seating around a central space, used for events such as drama or sports.

ANCESTORS
People from whom another person is descended.

ANIMISM
A religious belief that everything on Earth is imbued with a spirit.

ANTHROPOLOGISTS
People who study and compare human societies and cultures.

ASTRONOMICAL CLOCK
A clock that shows the positions of the Sun, Moon, planets, and large constellations of stars.

AVALANCHES
Large bodies of snow, ice, and rocks falling rapidly down a mountainside.

BAUXITE
A clayey rock from which aluminum is mined.

BIODIVERSITY
The variety of plant and animal life in a particular place.

CARBON DIOXIDE
A colorless gas found in the atmosphere, which is given off when humans breathe out.

CARGO
Goods carried on a ship, airplane, or in a motor vehicle.

CARNIVOROUS
Describes animals that eat only meat.

CONTINENTAL DRIFT
The gradual movement of the continents across the Earth's surface.

CONURBATION
A large urban area in which several towns merge with the suburbs of a central city.

COSMOPOLITAN
Describes something, such as a city, with many different people and cultures.

CREMATE
To burn a dead person's body.

DEHYDRATION
When the body loses a lot of water. Dehydration can cause a dry, sticky mouth, sleepiness, and can lead to vomiting and death.

ELEVATION
The height of a mountain.

EROSION
The gradual wearing away of something by water, wind, or ice.

EUROPEAN UNION (EU)
An economic and political union of 27 countries within Europe.

EXPEDITION
A journey undertaken by a team or group of people to discover and explore a new place.

EXTINCT
Describes a plant or animal that no longer survives. For example, the Arctic reindeer is extinct.

FAUNA
Animals.

FERTILE
Land of a quality on which crops can be grown.

FLORA
Plants.

FOLD MOUNTAINS
Mountains that are formed when two tectonic plates are pushed together.

FOSSIL
Describes something that has become preserved in rock, or fossilized.

GENETICALLY MODIFIED
Describes something that has been changed by scientists to produce certain characteristics. For example, animals can be injected with hormones to produce more meat.

GLACIER
A slowly moving mass or river of ice.

HEATWAVE
Abnormally hot weather for a long period of time.

HERBIVORES
Animals, such as elephants and giraffes, that eat only plants.

HIV
Short for the human immunodeficiency virus. This is the virus that causes AIDS, an illness that can be fatal.

HUNTER-GATHERER
A person who lives by hunting, fishing, and harvesting wild food.

ICE CAP
A covering of ice over a large area, usually at the Poles.

ICEBERG
A large floating piece of ice that has been carried out to sea.

IMMIGRANTS
People from a different country.

IMPORT
To bring goods into a country.

INDUSTRIALIZE
To develop industries on a large scale.

INSCRIPTIONS
Something "written" on a monument.

LAVA
Hot molten or semifluid rock that has erupted from a volcano.

LIMESTONE
A hard rock used in building.

LUNAR CALENDAR
A calendar based on the phases of the Moon.

MARSUPIAL
A mammal, usually found in Australia, whose young are carried in a pouch on the mother's belly.

MAUSOLEUM
A large building that houses a tomb or several tombs.

MIGRATE
To move from one country or region to another.

MUDSLIDES
A mass of mud that has fallen down a hillside or other slope.

NICKEL
A silvery-white metal.

NOCTURNAL
Describes animals, such as owls, that are active mainly at night.

NOMADIC
Describes people that travel from place to place.

NUCLEAR POWER
Electricity generated from a nuclear reactor.

OTTOMAN EMPIRE
A Turkish empire that lasted from the end of the thirteenth century to the beginning of the twentieth century.

OUTBACK
The inland areas of Australia where very few people live.

OZONE LAYER
A layer of gases around the Earth that absorbs most of the radiation reaching the Earth from the Sun.

PADDIES
Fields where rice is grown.

PAPYRUS
A water plant used in ancient Egypt to make paper.

PERMAFROST
A thick layer of soil that remains frozen throughout the year.

PHARAOH
A ruler of ancient Egypt.

PLATEAU
A flat area of land that is usually at a high altitude.

PLATINUM
A precious silvery-white metal.

POLYTHEISM
The belief in or worship of more than one god.

RENAISSANCE
The growth of European art and literature from the fourteenth to the sixteenth century.

RENEWABLE ENERGY
Energy from a source that will not run out, such as the Sun.

SARCOPHAGUS
A stone coffin.

SCANDINAVIAN
Describes someone or something from Scandinavia (Norway, Sweden, and Denmark).

SCAVENGERS
Animals, such as hyenas, that feed on dead animals, plant material, or refuse.

SOLAR POWER
Electricity generated by harnessing the Sun's energy.

SYMMETRICAL
Describes something made up of exactly the same parts facing each other.

TECTONIC PLATES
Pieces of the Earth's crust and upper mantle.

TERRACED GARDEN
A garden that has steps or raised areas.

TITANIUM
A hard silver-gray metal.

TRIBUTARY
A river or stream flowing into a larger river or lake.

TROPICAL STORM
A storm that has thunderstorms, very strong winds, and brings with it heavy rain.

URANIUM
A silvery-white metal, used to create nuclear power.

URBANIZATION
The process whereby a place becomes more urban or city-like.

VIADUCT
A bridge made up of several small spans.

INDEX

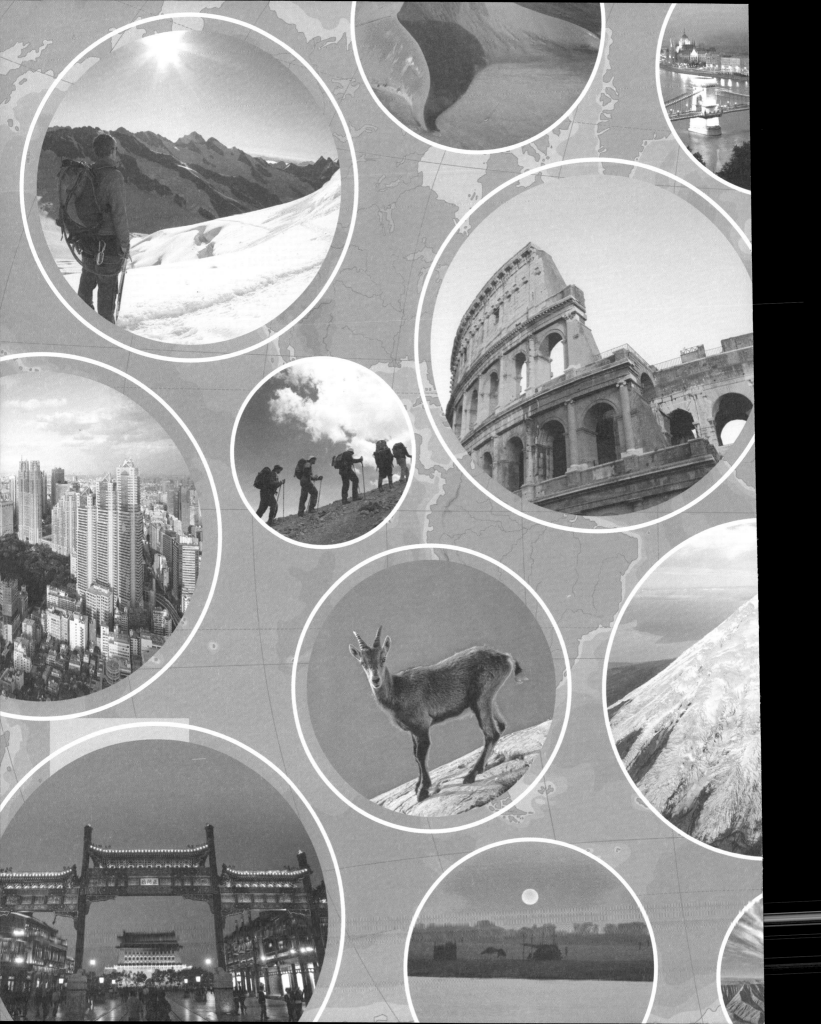